Introduction

"The Perfect Cake" is an extraordinary cookbook that delves into the art of cake baking, guiding you on a journey to create exquisite and unforgettable confections. With its meticulous attention to detail and expert techniques, this cookbook empowers both novice and seasoned bakers to master the craft of cake making.

Inside "The Perfect Cake," you'll find an enchanting collection of recipes that have been carefully curated to ensure exceptional results every time. From classic flavors to innovative combinations, each recipe has been perfected to achieve a harmonious balance of taste and texture. Explore a world of cakes, from elegant layer cakes and show-stopping celebration cakes to delightful cupcakes and indulgent tortes.

Beyond its delectable recipes, "The Perfect Cake" serves as a comprehensive baking guide. It provides insights into essential techniques, such as achieving the perfect crumb, mastering buttercream frosting, and creating intricate decorations. With step-by-step instructions, helpful tips, and beautiful photographs, this cookbook equips you with the knowledge and confidence to create cakes that are as visually stunning as they are delicious.

"The Perfect Cake" also celebrates the joy of personalization and creativity. Discover inspirations for flavor variations, decorative finishes, and unique presentations that will make your cakes truly stand out. Whether you're baking for a special occasion or simply indulging in a well-deserved treat, this cookbook invites you to unleash your imagination and create cakes that are a true reflection of your passion for baking.

Easy Carrot Cake

Ingredients
230ml vegetable oil, plus extra for the tin
100g natural yogurt
4 large eggs
1½ tsp vanilla extract
½ orange, zested
265g self-raising flour
335g light muscovado sugar
2½ tsp ground cinnamon
¼ fresh nutmeg, finely grated
265g carrots (about 3), grated
100g sultanas or raisins
100g walnuts or pecans, roughly chopped (optional)
For the icing
100g slightly salted butter, softened
300g icing sugar
100g soft cheese

Method

Heat the oven to 180C/160C fan/gas 4. Oil and line the base and sides of two 20cm cake tins with baking parchment. Whisk the oil, yogurt, eggs, vanilla and zest in a jug. Mix the flour, sugar, cinnamon and nutmeg with a good pinch of salt in a bowl. Squeeze any lumps of sugar through your fingers, shaking the bowl a few times to bring the lumps to the surface.

Add the wet ingredients to the dry, along with the carrots, raisins and half the nuts, if using. Mix well to combine, then divide between the tins.

Bake for 25-30 mins or until a skewer inserted into the centre of the cake comes out clean. If any wet mixture clings to the skewer, return to the oven for 5 mins, then check again. Leave to cool in the tins.

To make the icing, beat the butter and sugar together until smooth. Add half the soft cheese and beat again, then add the rest (adding it bit by bit prevents the icing from splitting). Remove the cakes from the tins and sandwich together with half the icing. Top with the remaining icing and scatter with the remaining walnuts. Will keep in the fridge for up to five days. Best eaten at room temperature.

Easy Lemon Cake

Ingredients
225g <u>unsalted butter</u>, softened
225g <u>caster sugar</u>
4 large <u>eggs</u>
225g <u>self-raising flour</u>
1 tsp <u>baking powder</u>
75g <u>natural yogurt</u>
1 tsp <u>vanilla bean paste</u> or extract
3 <u>lemons</u>, zested
For the drizzle
150g <u>granulated sugar</u>
3 <u>lemons</u>, zest of 2 pared into strips, juiced
(you'll need 60ml)
For the icing
150g <u>unsalted butter</u>, softened
150g <u>icing sugar</u>, sieved
1 tsp <u>vanilla bean paste</u> or extract
300g full-fat soft cheese

Method

Heat the oven to 180C/160C fan/gas 4 and line the base of two 20cm sandwich tins with baking parchment. Beat the butter and sugar together for 3 mins using an electric <u>whisk</u> until smooth and fluffy. Add the eggs, one at a time, beating well between each addition and scraping down the sides of the bowl. Fold in the flour and baking powder until well incorporated, then fold in the yogurt, vanilla and lemon zest. Divide between the tins and bake for 30-35 mins until golden and a skewer inserted into the middles comes out clean.

Meanwhile, make the drizzle. Tip the sugar, lemon juice and 100ml water into a small pan set over a medium heat and stir until dissolved. Add the lemon zest, bring to the boil and simmer for 2-3 mins until the zest has softened and the liquid is syrupy. Remove the zest to a sheet of baking parchment using a slotted spoon, and remove the syrup from the heat.

Leave the sponges to cool for 10 mins in the tins, then pour over the warm drizzle. Leave to cool completely.

For the icing, beat the butter and icing sugar together using an electric whisk for 4-5 mins until smooth, scraping down the sides of the bowl as you go. Add the vanilla and soft cheese and beat for 4 mins more until thick and creamy. Don't worry if it doesn't look thick at first – it will loosen, then thicken again as you beat it.

Remove the cooled sponges from the tins. Spoon the icing into a <u>piping bag</u> fitted with a star nozzle. Put one sponge on a cake stand or serving plate, and pipe just under half the icing around the edge using a circular motion for a wavy effect. Pipe a little more icing over the empty middle (this doesn't need to be neat) and smooth with the back of a spoon. Chill for 45 mins-1 hr until set. Top with the second sponge, then pipe eight blobs of icing around the edge at regular intervals, leaving a gap between each. Spoon the candied lemon zest into each gap, then serve.

Blackberry and Orange Cake

Ingredients

225g <u>unsalted butter</u>, softened, plus extra for the tins
225g <u>caster sugar</u>
4 <u>large eggs</u>
1tsp <u>vanilla extract</u>
250g <u>self-raising flour</u>
1tsp <u>baking powder</u>
2 <u>oranges</u>, zested (reserve the oranges for the drizzle, below)
150g <u>blackberries</u>, halved if large
For the drizzle
3 <u>oranges</u>, juiced (use the zested oranges, above, you'll need about 150ml), 1 zested
100g <u>caster sugar</u>
For the topping
150g <u>unsalted butter</u>, softened
350g <u>icing sugar</u>
1 <u>orange</u>, zested, plus extra zest to serve
1tbsp <u>milk</u>
200g marmalade
100g <u>blackberries</u>

Method

Heat the oven to 180C/160C fan/ gas 4. Butter two 20cm loose-bottomed cake tins and line with baking parchment. Beat the butter and caster sugar together in a large <u>bowl</u> using an electric <u>whisk</u> until pale and fluffy. Add the eggs, one at a time, until combined. Tip in the vanilla, flour and baking powder and fold until smooth, then gently fold in the orange zest and blackberries, being careful not to overmix.

Divide the batter between the two tins and bake for 35-40 mins until golden and a skewer inserted into the middles comes out clean. Cover with foil after 30 mins if they start to colour too quickly.

Meanwhile, make the drizzle. Put the orange juice, zest and sugar in a small pan and simmer for 4-5 mins until a thin syrup forms. Pour into a heatproof bowl and set aside.

When the sponges are ready, drizzle the syrup over both while still warm and brush over evenly using a pastry brush. Leave to cool completely in the tins.

Meanwhile, make the buttercream for the topping. Beat the butter and icing sugar in a large bowl with an electric whisk until light, pale and fluffy. Whisk in the orange zest and milk until loosened slightly. Spoon into a <u>piping bag</u> fitted with a large round nozzle. Beat the marmalade to loosen, then transfer a little to a piping bag fitted with a small round nozzle.

Remove the cooled sponges from the tins, and place one on a cake board or plate. Pipe buttercream dots on top in a circle around the edge, then three dots in the middle. Spoon some marmalade into the gaps between the buttercream, then top with the second sponge. Pipe more buttercream dots all over the surface, then fill in the gaps by piping in the remaining marmalade. To finish, scatter with the blackberries and extra orange zest.

Citrus, Almond and Yogurt Cake

Ingredients
165g <u>butter</u>, plus extra for the tin
200g <u>golden caster sugar</u>, plus 2 tbsp
150g <u>self-raising flour</u>
100g <u>ground almonds</u>
3 <u>eggs</u>
75g <u>natural yogurt</u>, plus 2 tbsp
1 large <u>lemon</u>
1 <u>orange</u>
100g <u>icing sugar</u>
15g toasted flaked <u>almonds</u>

Method

Melt the butter in a small pan. Remove from the heat and leave to cool slightly. Meanwhile, butter a 23cm springform cake tin and line with baking parchment. Heat the oven to 180C/160C fan/gas 4.

Put the 200g caster sugar, flour and ground almonds in a large <u>bowl</u> and mix well. <u>Whisk</u> the eggs and 75g yogurt into the cooled melted butter, then pour this into the bowl with the dry ingredients. Zest the lemon and orange over the bowl. Stir with a <u>spatula</u> until there are no streaks of flour, then scrape into the tin and bake on the middle shelf of the oven for 40 mins.

Cut a few slices each from the zested lemon and orange, then squeeze the juice from what's left of each into a saucepan (you'll need about 6 tbsp total). Add the 2 tbsp caster sugar and the fruit slices to the pan. Bring to the boil and cook for 5-10 mins, or until the juice has reduced to a thin syrup and the fruit slices have softened. Leave to cool. Remove the fruit slices to a sheet of baking parchment and leave to dry.

Insert a skewer into the middle of the cake – it should come out dry, with no wet cake mix clinging to it. If it's not ready, bake for 5-10 mins more and check again. Leave to cool in the tin for 5 mins, then spoon over the citrus syrup. Leave to cool for 10 mins more, then remove from the tin. To freeze, first leave to cool completely, then wrap the cake well. Will keep frozen for up to three months.

Mix the 2 tbsp yogurt with the icing sugar to make a thick icing. Spoon this onto the centre of the cake and use the back of a spoon to ease it to the edge (it should drip over the side). Scatter over the flaked almonds and decorate with the fruit slices. Serve warm, or leave to cool completely. Will keep in an airtight tin for up to five days.

Easy Chocolate Cake

Ingredients

150ml <u>sunflower oil</u>, plus extra for the tin
175g <u>self-raising flour</u>
2 tbsp cocoa powder
1 tsp <u>bicarbonate of soda</u>
150g <u>caster sugar</u>
2 tbsp <u>golden syrup</u>
2 <u>large eggs</u>, lightly beaten
150ml semi-skimmed milk
For the icing
100g <u>unsalted butter</u>
225g <u>icing sugar</u>
40g cocoa powder
2½ tbsp <u>milk</u> (a little more if needed)

Method

Heat the oven to 180C/160C fan/gas 4. Oil and line the base of two 18cm sandwich tins. Sieve the flour, cocoa powder and bicarbonate of soda into a bowl. Add the caster sugar and mix well.

Make a well in the centre and add the golden syrup, eggs, sunflower oil and milk. Beat well with an electric whisk until smooth.

Pour the mixture into the two tins and bake for 25-30 mins until risen and firm to the touch. Remove from oven, leave to cool for 10 mins before turning out onto a cooling rack.

To make the icing, beat the unsalted butter in a bowl until soft. Gradually sieve and beat in the icing sugar and cocoa powder, then add enough of the milk to make the icing fluffy and spreadable.

Sandwich the two cakes together with the butter icing and cover the sides and the top of the cake with more icing.

Caramel Cake

Ingredients
225g softened salted butter, plus extra for
the tins
125g golden caster sugar
100g light brown soft sugar
1 tsp vanilla extract
4 large eggs
225g self raising flour
2 tbsp milk
toffee, chocolate or caramel pieces, to
decorate
For the icing
200g softened salted butter
400g icing sugar (golden icing sugar if you
can find it – it adds a golden colour and
caramel flavour)
70g caramel sauce, dulce de leche or
caramel spread, plus 3 tbsp to serve

Method

Heat the oven to 180C/160C fan/gas 4. Butter two 20cm springform tins and line the bases with baking parchment.

Beat the butter and both sugars in a bowl with an electric whisk for a few mins until lighter in colour and fluffy. Add the vanilla and the eggs, one at a time, adding a spoonful of flour and beating in between each egg. Add the remaining flour and milk. Divide between the cake tins and bake for 25-30 mins until they're golden, spring back when pressed, and a skewer comes out clean when inserted into the middle. Cool in the tins for a few mins, then tip out and leave to cool completely on a wire rack.

Meanwhile, for the icing, put the butter and icing sugar in a bowl and whisk for a few mins until light and airy. Whisk in the caramel briefly, adding 1 tbsp of boiling water to loosen, if needed. Set aside until the sponges are completely cool before assembling, or the icing will melt.

Use half the icing to sandwich the cakes together, then spread the remainder over the top, smoothing it out with a knife or the back of a spoon. Leave in a cool place until ready to serve. Drizzle with the 3 tbsp extra sauce (warm briefly in the microwave if it's a little stiff), allowing some to drip down the sides if you like, and scatter over the toffee, chocolate or caramel pieces to serve. Edible glitter, birthday candles or sparklers, optional.

Coffee and Walnut Cake

Ingredients

250g <u>pack softened butter,</u> plus extra for the tins
100ml strong black coffee (made with 2 tbsp coffee
granules), cooled
280g <u>self-raising flour</u>
250g <u>golden caster sugar</u>
½ tsp <u>baking powder</u>
4 <u>eggs</u>
1 tsp <u>vanilla extract</u>
85g <u>walnut,</u> 2 tbsp roughly chopped, the rest
finely chopped
For the filling
100g <u>icing sugar,</u> sifted, plus a little extra for
dusting
150ml <u>double cream</u>
100g mascarpone, at room temperature

Method

Heat oven to 180C/160C fan/gas 4. Butter 2 x 20cm springform cake tins and line with baking parchment. Set aside 2 tbsp of the coffee for the filling.

STEP 2. sugar, baking powder, eggs, vanilla and half the remaining coffee in a large bowl with an electric whisk until lump-free. Fold in the finely chopped walnuts, then divide between the tins and roughly spread. Scatter the roughly chopped walnuts over one of the cakes. Bake the cakes for 25-30 mins until golden and risen, and a skewer poked in comes out clean. Drizzle the plain cake with the remaining coffee. Cool the cakes in the tins.

Meanwhile, make the filling: beat together the icing sugar, cream and mascarpone, then fold in the reserved 2 tbsp coffee. Spread over the plain cake, then cover with the walnut-topped cake and dust with a little icing sugar.

Red Velvet Cake

Ingredients:
1 ½ cups white sugar
½ cup shortening
2 eggs
4 tablespoons red food coloring
2 tablespoons cocoa
1 cup buttermilk
1 teaspoon salt
1 teaspoon vanilla extract
2 ½ cups sifted all-purpose flour
1 tablespoon distilled white vinegar
1 ½ teaspoons baking soda

Icing:
1 cup milk
5 tablespoons all-purpose flour
1 cup white sugar
1 cup butter, room temperature
1 teaspoon vanilla extract

Preheat the oven to 350 degrees F (175 degrees C). Grease two 9-inch round pans.

Make the cake: Beat 1 1/2 cups sugar and shortening together in a large bowl with an electric mixer until light and fluffy. Add eggs one at a time, beating well after each addition. Combine red food coloring and cocoa to make a paste; add to creamed mixture.

Mix buttermilk, salt, and 1 teaspoon vanilla together in a small bowl. Add flour, alternating with buttermilk mixture, mixing just until incorporated. Mix vinegar and baking soda together; gently fold into cake batter and pour into prepared pans.

Bake in the preheated oven until a toothpick inserted into the center comes out clean, about 30 minutes. Cool on a wire rack for 5 minutes. Run a table knife around the edges to loosen. Invert carefully onto a serving plate or cooling rack. Let cool, about 30 minutes.

Make the icing: Heat milk and flour in a saucepan over low heat, stirring constantly, until thick. Set aside to cool completely.

Meanwhile, beat sugar, butter, and vanilla together in a large bowl with an electric mixer until light and fluffy. Add cooled flour mixture and beat until frosting is a good spreading consistency. Frost cake layers when completely cool.

Vanilla Cake

Ingredients
cooking spray

2 ⅔ cups all-purpose flour, or more as
needed

1 cup white sugar

1 tablespoon baking powder

1 tablespoon vanilla extract

2 pinches salt

3 eggs

¾ cup milk

¾ cup vegetable oil

Preheat the oven to 350 degrees F (175 degrees C). Grease a 9-inch cake tin
with cooking spray and line with parchment paper.

Mix flour, sugar, baking powder, vanilla extract, and salt together in a large
bowl. Add eggs, milk, and vegetable oil; mix by hand or beat with an
electric mixer on low speed until smooth. Add more flour if batter is too
runny. Pour into the prepared pan.

Bake in the preheated oven until a toothpick inserted into the center of the
cake comes out clean, about 1 hour. Cool on a wire rack for 5 minutes. Run
a table knife around the edges to loosen. Invert cake carefully onto a
cooling rack. Let cool completely.

Black Forest Cake

Ingredients:
2 ⅛ cups all-purpose flour

2 cups white sugar

¾ cup unsweetened cocoa powder

1 ½ teaspoons baking powder

¾ teaspoon baking soda

¾ teaspoon salt. 3 eggs. .1 cup milk

½ cup vegetable oil

1 tablespoon vanilla extract

Topping:
2 (20 ounce) cans pitted sour cherries

1 cup white sugar .¼ cup cornstarch

1 teaspoon vanilla extract

Frosting:
3 cups heavy whipping cream

⅓ cup confectioners' sugar

Preheat the oven to 350 degrees F (175 degrees C). Grease and flour two 9-inch round cake pans; line bottoms with parchment paper. Place a medium bowl in the refrigerator to chill.

Whisk flour, sugar, cocoa, baking powder, baking soda, and salt together in a large bowl. Add eggs, milk, oil, and vanilla; beat until combined. Pour cake batter into the prepared pans.

Bake in the preheated oven until a toothpick inserted in the centers comes out clean, about 35 minutes. Cool layers in pans on wire racks for 10 minutes. Run a paring knife around edges to loosen and invert carefully onto racks to cool completely, 1 to 2 hours.

While cake layers bake, drain cherries for topping, reserving 1/2 cup juice. Combine reserved juice, cherries, sugar, and cornstarch in a 2-quart saucepan. Cook, stirring constantly, over low heat until thickened. Stir in vanilla. Let cool at room temperature for 30 minutes. Transfer to the refrigerator to cool completely before assembling cake.

Combine whipping cream and confectioners' sugar for frosting in the chilled medium bowl. Beat with an electric mixer at high speed until stiff peaks form.

Split each cake layer in half horizontally using a long serrated knife. Tear one layer into crumbs; set aside. Gently brush loose crumbs off top and sides of remaining layers using a pastry brush or your hands. Reserve 1 1/2 cups frosting for piping decorations on cake; set aside.

To assemble, place one cake layer on a cake plate. Spread with 1 cup frosting; top with 3/4 cup cherry topping. Top with second cake layer; repeat layers of frosting and cherry topping. Top with third cake layer and frost sides of cake.

Pat reserved cake crumbs onto sides of cake. Spoon reserved 1 1/2 cups frosting into a pastry bag fitted with a star decorator tip. Pipe around top and bottom edges of cake. Spoon remaining cherry topping on top of cake.

Store covered in the refrigerator until ready to serve.

Checkerboard Cake

Ingredients

1 (15.25 ounce) package devil's food cake mix (such as Duncan Hines®)
2 cups whole milk, divided
⅔ cup salted butter, melted, divided
3 large eggs
2 teaspoons vanilla extract, divided
Baking spray with flour
1 (15.25 ounce) package white cake mix (such as Duncan Hines®)
3 large egg whites

Frosting:
½ cup salted butter, softened
1 (8 ounce) package cream cheese, softened
1 (32 ounce) package powdered sugar
½ cup unsweetened cocoa powder
4 tablespoons whole milk, or more as needed
2 teaspoons vanilla extract

Prepare cakes: Preheat the oven to 350 degrees F (175 degrees C) with racks in middle and lower third positions.

Place devil's food cake mix, 1 cup milk, 1/3 cup melted butter, 3 large eggs, and 1 teaspoon vanilla extract in the bowl of a stand mixer. Beat at low speed, using the paddle attachment, for 1 minute until combined. Increase speed to medium and beat for 2 minutes.

Spoon batter evenly into 2 (9-inch) round nonstick cake pans, greased with baking spray; set aside.
Repeat procedure with the white cake mix, substituting 3 egg whites for 3 large eggs.
Bake 4 cakes in the preheated oven until a wooden pick inserted in middle comes out clean, 20 to 25 minutes, rotating cake pans from front to back and between top and bottom racks halfway through baking time.

Remove pans to a wire rack and cool for 10 minutes. Remove cakes from pans and cool completely on wire racks, about 1 hour.
Trim the top of the cakes as needed to make sure the top is level.

Prepare frosting: Beat softened butter with a stand mixer at medium speed, using the paddle attachment, until creamy, 1 to 2 minutes.
Add softened cream cheese and mix for 1 minute until combined, stopping to scrape down sides of bowl as needed.
Whisk together powdered sugar and cocoa in a large bowl; gradually add to butter mixture alternately with 4 tablespoons milk, along with the vanilla. Beat at low speed until blended after each addition, stopping to scrape down bowl in between additions. (If needed, add up to 1 tablespoon milk, 1 teaspoon at a time, to reach desired consistency.) Increase speed to medium, and beat 1 to 2 minutes or until light and fluffy.
Assemble cake: Place 1 chocolate cake layer on a cutting board. Using a 6-inch round cutter, cut out center of cake to create a 6-inch cake round; leave 9-inch cake ring intact, and remove center 6-inch cake. Using a 3-inch round cutter, cut out center of the 6-inch cake to create a 3-inch cake round; leave 6-inch ring intact, and remove center 3-inch cake round. Place the 9-inch cake ring on a serving platter or cake stand. Set aside 6-inch ring and 3-inch cake round.
Repeat process with 1 vanilla cake layer to create 1 (9-inch) vanilla cake ring, 1 (6-inch) vanilla cake ring, and 1 (3-inch) vanilla cake round.
Place the 6-inch vanilla ring in the center of the 9-inch chocolate ring. Place the 3-inch chocolate cake round in the center of the 6-inch vanilla ring.
Spread a thin layer of frosting over layer on platter. Place 9-inch vanilla cake ring on frosted layer and place the 6-inch chocolate ring in center of thee 9-inch vanilla ring. Place the 3-inch vanilla cake round in the center of the 6-inch chocolate ring. Spread a thin layer of frosting over layer. Repeat process with remaining chocolate cake layer and vanilla cake layer.
Spread remaining frosting over top and sides of cake. Chill for 15 minutes before serving.

Bananas Cake

Ingredients

cooking spray
2 ½ cups all-purpose flour
2 teaspoons baking soda
1 teaspoon table salt
2 cups granulated sugar
2 cups mashed banana (from 5 (6 oz.) bananas)
1 cup canola oil
¾ cup plain whole Greek yogurt
¼ cup whole buttermilk
2 teaspoons vanilla extract
2 large eggs

Salted Banana Caramel Sauce
1 cup dark brown sugar
½ cup heavy cream
⅓ cup unsalted butter
¾ teaspoon ground cinnamon
¼ teaspoon sea salt
1 ½ very ripe bananas, mashed
¾ teaspoon vanilla bean paste or 1 1/2 vanilla beans
4 tablespoons dark rum (such as Meyer's dark rum), divided
3 ripe bananas, sliced

Caramel Frosting
2 cups unsalted butter, softened
4 cups powdered sugar
1 cup salted banana caramel sauce

Preheat oven to 350 degrees F (175 degrees C). Spray 3 (8-inch) round cake pans with cooking spray, and line bottoms with parchment.

Whisk together flour, baking soda, and salt in a large bowl. Whisk together sugar, 2 cups mashed banana, oil, yogurt, buttermilk, vanilla, and eggs in a second bowl until well blended; add to flour mixture and stir just until combined. Divide batter evenly between prepared pans.

Bake in the preheated oven until a toothpick is inserted and comes out clean, 25 to 30 minutes. Cool in pans on a wire rack for 10 minutes. Remove cakes from pans to a wire rack cool completely, about 1 to1/2 hours.
Meanwhile for the caramel sauce, combine sugar, cream, butter, cinnamon and salt in a small saucepan. Cook over medium heat, whisking constantly, until butter is melted and sugar is dissolved, about 2 minutes. Whisk in 1 1/2 mashed banana, vanilla bean paste, and 3 tablespoons of the rum and remove from heat.

Place sliced bananas in a small bowl and drizzle with 4 tablespoons of the caramel sauce and remaining 1 tablespoon rum; toss gently to coat. Cool remaining caramel sauce to room temperature, about 20 minutes.

For the caramel frosting, beat butter in the bowl of a stand mixer fitted with the paddle attachment on medium speed until light in color, about 3 minutes. Gradually add powdered sugar, and beat on medium speed for about 3 minutes until light and fluffy. Add 1 cup of the salted banana caramel sauce, and beat on low speed until combined, about 1 minute. Transfer 1 cup frosting to a piping bag fitted with a #12 tip. To assemble the cake, place 1 cake layer on a serving plate; spread with 2/3 cup Caramel Frosting. Using the piping bag to pipe a ring of Caramel Frosting around outer edge of cake layer on top of frosting.

Spoon half of sliced banana mixture inside frosting ring and spread evenly. Top with second cake layer.

Spread another 2/3 cup caramel frosting over second layer. Repeat with piping bag to pipe a ring of caramel frosting around outer edge of cake layer on top of frosting.

Spoon remaining sliced banana mixture inside frosting ring and spread evenly. Top with remaining cake layer.
Spread remaining frosting on top and sides of cake and smooth.
Use piping bag to decorate as desired.
Slice and serve with remaining 3/4 cup caramel sauce.

Watermelon Cake

Ingredients

nonstick baking spray
2 ½ cups all-purpose flour
1 tablespoon all-purpose flour
3 tablespoons watermelon-flavored gelatin mix (such as Jell-O®)
1 teaspoon baking powder
1 teaspoon kosher salt
½ teaspoon baking soda
1 cup unsalted butter, softened
2 cups white sugar
3 large eggs
1 ½ cups whole buttermilk
2 teaspoons vanilla extract
1 teaspoon red gel food coloring
1 cup miniature semisweet chocolate chips

Frosting:
1 ½ cups unsalted butter, softened
¼ teaspoon kosher salt
2 teaspoons vanilla extract
6 cups powdered sugar
6 tablespoons heavy whipping cream
red food coloring gel
green food coloring gel
miniature semisweet chocolate chips for decoration

Preheat oven to 350 degrees F (175 degrees C). Coat three 8-inch round cake pans with baking spray; set aside.

Whisk together 2 1/2 cups flour, gelatin, baking powder, salt, and baking soda in a medium bowl.

Beat butter at medium speed with a stand mixer, fitted with the paddle attachment, until creamy, about 3 minutes. Gradually add sugar, beating until light and fluffy, 3 to 4 minutes. Add eggs, 1 at a time, beating just until blended and stopping to scrape down sides of bowl after each addition. Add flour mixture to butter mixture alternately with buttermilk, beginning and ending with flour mixture, beating at low speed until just blended after each addition.

Beat in vanilla and red food coloring gel until blended. Toss chocolate chips with remaining 1 tablespoon flour in a small bowl. Gently fold into batter. Divide batter evenly among prepared cake pans.
Bake in the preheated oven until a wooden pick inserted in the center comes out clean, 28 to 32 minutes.

Cool in pans on a wire rack for 10 minutes. Remove cakes from pans and cool completely on wire rack about 1 hour.
Prepare Frosting: Beat butter and salt with a stand mixer fitted with a paddle attachment on medium speed until creamy, about 3 minutes; beat in vanilla.
Gradually add powdered sugar alternately with 6 tablespoons cream, beating on low speed, until completely incorporated and smooth, about 2 minutes. Increase mixer speed to medium-high and beat until mixture is smooth and fluffy, about 2 to 3 minutes.

Remove 1/3 cup of the frosting to a small bowl. Remove 2 cups of the frosting to a medium bowl; stir in enough red food coloring until desired shade of red. Tint remaining frosting with green food coloring gel until desired shade of green.
Assemble Cake: Place 1 cake layer on a serving platter or cake stand. Spread top with 2/3 cup red frosting. Top with a second cake layer; spread top with 2/3 cup red frosting. Top with remaining cake layer; spread top with remaining red frosting, leaving a 1/2-inch border around edge.
Frost sides of cake with green frosting. Place reserved 1/3 cup plain frosting into a piping bag or zip-lock bag with a 1/4-inch hole cut in the corner.
Pipe plain frosting around top edge of cake, filling in the 1/4-inch border.

Sprinkle top with miniature chocolate chips to resemble seeds.

S'mores Cake

Ingredients

baking spray
1 (15.25 ounce) package dark chocolate cake mix (such as
Betty Crocker® Super Moist®)
3 large eggs
1 cup whole milk
⅓ cup melted unsalted butter
1 tablespoon instant espresso powder
3 teaspoons vanilla extract, divided
1 (12 ounce) bag semi-sweet chocolate chips
1 ½ cups heavy whipping cream
5 large egg whites
1 ⅔ cups granulated sugar
½ teaspoon cream of tartar
¾ cup graham cracker crumbs, divided
10 small graham cracker rectangles

Gather all ingredients.

Preheat the oven to 350 degrees F (175 degrees C). Line the bottom of 2 (9-inch) cake pans with parchment paper, lightly spray with baking spray.

Combine cake mix, eggs, milk, and butter in a large bowl. Beat with an electric mixer until well combined. Mix in espresso powder and 2 teaspoons vanilla extract. Divide batter evenly between prepared pans, spreading into even layers.

Bake in the preheated oven until a wooden pick inserted into centers of cake comes out clean, 25 to 30 minutes. Cool cakes in pans on a wire rack for 20 minutes, then remove cakes from pans. Let cool completely on a wire rack, about 1 hour.

While cakes are baking, place chocolate chips into a heatproof bowl. Bring cream in a small saucepan to a gentle simmer over medium-low heat, stirring constantly, about 6 minutes. Pour hot cream over chocolate chips and let stand for 5 minutes. Gently stir together in a circular motion to evenly blend chocolate into cream, without adding a lot of air. Let chocolate mixture cool, uncovered, at room temperature, stirring occasionally, until thickened to spreadable consistency, about 1 1/2 hours.

Meanwhile, bring a small saucepan filled with 2 inches water to a simmer over medium-low heat. Beat together egg whites, sugar, and cream of tartar in a work bowl of a stand mixer fitted with a whisk attachment on medium speed until well combined, about 1 minute.

Place mixer bowl over simmering saucepan, ensuring the bottom of the mixing bowl does not touch the water. Cook egg white mixture, whisking constantly, until a candy thermometer reaches 160 degrees F (70 degrees C) and the sugar crystals have dissolved, 8 to 10 minutes. Remove bowl from heat, and return to stand mixer. Beat on high speed, gradually adding remaining 1 teaspoon vanilla. Beat until stiff peaks form, 6 to 7 minutes.

Set aside 2 cups of marshmallow cream. Place remaining marshmallow cream into a piping bag fitted with a large star tip.

Remove cooled cakes from pans and discard parchment. Using a serrated knife, trim the tops of the cooled cakes to create a level top; use excess cake for trifle or just eat.

Place 1 cake layer on a cake stand or plate, cut side up. Spread reserved 2 cups marshmallow cream in an even layer on cake top.

Sprinkle 1/2 cup of the graham cracker crumbs evenly over top.

Top with remaining cake layer, cut-side down. Fill in any empty spots in seams of cake layers using marshmallow cream in piping bag; smooth sides using an offset spatula. Refrigerate stacked cake, uncovered, for 30 minutes.

Spoon 1 1/4 cups cooled chocolate mixture over top of the stacked cake. Spread into an even layer using a large cake spatula, allowing excess to extend over the sides. Frost sides of cake using remaining chocolate mixture, smoothing into an even layer.

Using marshmallow cream in piping bag, pipe 10 large rosettes along the top, outside edge of the cake.

Sprinkle center of the cake with remaining 1/4 cup graham cracker crumbs.

Arrange graham cracker rectangles upright on the long sides of each rectangle in a spoke-wheel design inside rosette rings on top of cake. Pipe 1 large rosette in center of graham cracker spoke-wheel design. Refrigerate, uncovered, until ready to serve, at least 30 minutes or up to 48 hours.

Just before serving, use a kitchen torch to slightly brown marshmallow rosettes. Slice and serve cake.

Dulce de Leche Cake

Ingredients

baking spray
2 cups all-purpose flour
2 teaspoons baking powder
1 teaspoon salt
1 cup white sugar
¾ cup unsalted butter, softened
⅓ cup dulce de leche
1 teaspoon vanilla extract
3 large eggs, at room temperature
¾ cup whole milk
¾ cup chopped toasted hazelnuts

Glaze:

¼ cup dulce de leche
2 tablespoons whole milk

Frosting:

1 cup unsalted butter, softened
3 cups unsifted powdered sugar
½ teaspoon salt
½ cup dulce de leche
¼ fluid ounce dark rum (such as Myers's®) (Optional)

Preheat the oven to 350 degrees F (175 degrees C). Spray two 8-inch round cake pans with baking spray; set aside.

Whisk the flour with the baking powder and salt in a medium bowl until combined; set aside.

Add white sugar and butter to the bowl of a stand mixer fitted with a paddle attachment. Beat on medium-high until light and fluffy, 2 to 3 minutes. Add 1/3 cup dulce de leche and vanilla; beat until well combined, 30 seconds, scraping down sides of bowl as needed. Reduce speed to low and add eggs one at a time, beating until just blended after each addition, 45 seconds. Add flour mixture alternately with 3/4 cup milk, beginning and ending with flour mixture and beating on low just until combined after each addition.
Evenly divide cake batter between prepared pans.
Bake in the preheated oven until golden and a toothpick inserted in the center comes out clean, 25 to 30 minutes. Cool cakes in pans for 10 minutes.
Prepare the glaze: Whisk together 1/4 cup dulce de leche and 2 tablespoons milk until mixture is smooth.

Invert cakes from pans onto a wire cooling rack; set rack on a baking sheet. Using a wooden skewer or fork, gently poke holes all over flat sides (bottoms) of cakes. Pour dulce de leche glaze mixture over cakes and smooth with an offset spatula to coax mixture into holes. Let cool completely, about 30 minutes.
Prepare frosting: Beat butter in a stand mixer fitted with the paddle attachment on medium speed until smooth, about 1 minute. With mixer running on low speed, gradually add powdered sugar, beating until smooth, about 1 minute, stopping to scrape down sides of bowl as needed. Beat in salt. Increase speed to medium, and beat until fluffy, about 2 minutes. Scrape down sides of bowl, and beat in 1/2 cup dulce de leche and rum (if using) on low speed until just incorporated, 45 seconds.
Assemble the cake: Set a cake layer on a plate with the flat side (bottom) facing up. Evenly spread 1 cup of the frosting over the cake to the edge. Sprinkle with 1/4 cup of hazelnuts. Top with the second cake layer, rounded (top) side up. Spread the remaining frosting over the top and side of the cake. Sprinkle with remaining 1/2 cup of hazelnuts on top.

Strawberry Crunch Cake

Ingredients

baking spray with flour
2 ½ cups all-purpose flour
3 tablespoons strawberry-flavored gelatin, such as Jell-O (from 1 [3 oz.] package)
1 teaspoon baking powder
1 teaspoon kosher salt
½ teaspoon baking soda
1 cup unsalted butter, softened
2 cups granulated sugar
3 large eggs
2 teaspoons vanilla extract
1 ½ cups whole buttermilk

Frosting
1 ½ cups unsalted butter, softened
¼ teaspoon kosher salt
1 tablespoon vanilla extract
4 cups powdered sugar, sifted
2 tablespoons heavy cream, or more as needed

Crumble
25 golden Oreo cookies
⅔ cup freeze-dried strawberries
⅛ teaspoon kosher salt
4 tablespoons melted unsalted butter

Preheat the oven to 350 degrees F (175 degrees C). Coat 2 (8-inch) round cake pans with baking spray with flour and line bottoms with parchment.

Whisk together flour, gelatin, baking powder, salt, and baking soda in a bowl.

Beat butter at medium speed until creamy, 2 to 3 minutes in the bowl of a stand mixer fitted with the paddle attachment. Gradually add sugar, beating until light and fluffy, about 3 minutes. Add eggs, 1 at a time, beating on low speed and scraping down sides of bowl as needed, until just combined. Beat in vanilla.
Add flour mixture in 3 additions alternately with buttermilk, beginning and ending with flour mixture and beating on low speed just until combined after each addition. Divide batter evenly between prepared pans.

Bake in the preheated oven until a wooden pick inserted in center comes out clean, about 40 minutes.
Cool in pans on a wire rack for 10 minutes; remove cakes from pans and cool completely on a wire rack, 1 to 1 1/2 hours.

For the frosting, add butter and salt to the bowl of a stand mixer fitted with the paddle attachment. Beat on medium speed until creamy, about 3 minutes. Beat in vanilla.

Gradually add powdered sugar, alternately with cream, beating on low speed until completely incorporated and smooth. Increase mixer speed to medium-high and beat until smooth and fluffy, 2 to 3 minutes.
For the crumble, place cookies, strawberries, and salt in a food processor and pulse until slightly chunky (bits of strawberry and cookie should still be visible), about 12 pulses. Drizzle in butter and pulse about 5 times to combine.
Trim tops of cakes with a serrated knife if needed to make flat on top.

Place 1 cake layer on serving platter; spread evenly with 1 cup frosting. Top with remaining cake layer.
Spread top and sides of cake with the remaining frosting.
Sprinkle Crumble over top and sides of cake, pressing lightly to adhere until completely covered. Chill cake for 1 hour before slicing.

Nutella Chocolate Cake

Ingredients
Cake:

nonstick baking spray
2 cups all-purpose flour
2 cups white sugar
¾ cup unsweetened cocoa powder
2 teaspoons baking powder
1 ½ teaspoons baking soda
1 teaspoon salt
1 teaspoon instant espresso powder
1 cup milk
½ cup vegetable oil
2 eggs
2 teaspoons vanilla extract
1 cup boiling water
Whipped Chocolate Fudge Filling:
8 ounces bittersweet chocolate, finely chopped
¾ cup heavy whipping cream
1 tablespoon shortening

Nutella® Buttercream Frosting:
1 cup unsalted butter, at room temperature
2 cups confectioners' sugar
⅔ cup chocolate-hazelnut spread (such as Nutella®)
1 teaspoon vanilla extract
1 pinch kosher salt
2 tablespoons heavy whipping cream

Chocolate Drippys:
4 ounces bittersweet chocolate, chopped
¼ cup heavy whipping cream
½ tablespoon shortening

Preheat the oven to 350 degrees F (175 degrees C). Line the bottoms of three 8-inch cake pans with parchment paper and spray with baking spray.

Combine flour, sugar, cocoa, baking powder, baking soda, salt, and espresso powder in a large bowl and whisk until well combined. Add milk, vegetable oil, eggs, and 2 teaspoons vanilla extract to flour mixture and mix together using an electric mixer on medium speed until well combined. Reduce speed and carefully pour boiling water into cake batter. Beat on high speed for about 1 minute to add air to the batter. Distribute cake batter evenly between the prepared cake pans.

Bake in the preheated oven until a toothpick inserted into the center comes out clean, 30 to 35 minutes. Remove from the oven and cool on a wire rack for 10 minutes. Run a table knife around the edges to loosen. Invert cakes carefully onto serving plates or cooling racks. Let cool completely. Trim tops of cakes to level, if necessary.

Place 8 ounces chopped chocolate in the heatproof bowl of a stand mixer and set aside. Whisk together 3/4 cup cream and 1 tablespoon shortening in a small saucepan and bring to a boil over medium heat. Remove from heat and pour boiling mixture over chocolate and whisk until melted and smooth. Cool to room temperature. Beat using an electric mixer on high speed until chocolate mixture is lighter in color and fluffy in texture, about 1 minute. Immediately proceed to assemble the cake before the the whipped chocolate fudge filling hardens, which makes it difficult to spread.

To assemble the cake, place 1 cooled cake layer with the trimmed side up on a cake pan or serving plate. Spread 1/2 the whipped chocolate fudge filling evenly on top. Add the next layer and spread remaining chocolate fudge filling on top. Top with third layer, trimmed side down.

To prepare the buttercream frosting, use a stand mixer affixed with the paddle attachment. Beat together butter and confectioners' sugar on low speed until well blended. Add chocolate-hazelnut spread and increase the speed to medium. Beat for 2 minutes. Add 1 teaspoon vanilla extract and kosher salt and whip for an additional 30 seconds. Add 2 tablespoons heavy whipping cream and beat until the frosting lightens slightly in color and texture, about 1 more minute.

Frost entire cake with buttercream frosting and chill for at least 1 hour.

For the chocolate drippys, place 4 ounces chopped chocolate in the heatproof bowl of a stand mixer and set aside. Whisk together 1/4 cup cream and 1/2 tablespoon shortening in a small saucepan and bring to a boil over medium heat. Pour boiling cream mixture over chocolate and whisk until melted and smooth. Let cool slightly, then pour mixture into a clean squeeze bottle. Let set until it has the consistency of thin ranch dressing. Squeeze on top of the frosted cake and allow to drip down the sides. Chill until chocolate is set. Decorate the top of the cake with assorted confections of your choice and serve at room temperature.

Tips
You can butter and lightly flour the baking pans instead of using parchment paper and baking spray.

Roasted Strawberry Sheet Cake

Ingredients:
For the roasted strawberries:

2 cups fresh strawberries, hulled and halved
2 tablespoons granulated sugar

For the cake:

2 cups all-purpose flour
1 1/2 teaspoons baking powder
1/2 teaspoon baking soda
1/2 teaspoon salt
1/2 cup unsalted butter, softened 1 cup granulated sugar
2 large eggs
1 teaspoon vanilla extract
1 cup buttermilk

For the cream cheese frosting:

8 ounces cream cheese, softened 1/2 cup unsalted butter, softened 3 cups powdered sugar
1 teaspoon vanilla extract
1-2 tablespoons milk, as needed

Instructions:

Preheat the oven to 375°F.
To make the roasted strawberries, toss the strawberries and sugar together in a bowl. Spread them in a single layer on a baking sheet lined with parchment paper. Roast for 15-20 minutes or until they are soft and fragrant. Remove from oven and set aside to cool.
In a medium mixing bowl, whisk together flour, baking powder, baking soda, and salt.
In a separate large mixing bowl, cream together butter and sugar until light and fluffy. Add eggs one at a time, mixing well after each addition. Stir in vanilla extract.
Add the dry ingredients to the wet ingredients, alternating with the buttermilk. Begin and end with the dry ingredients, mixing until just combined.
Fold in the roasted strawberries, reserving a few for topping.
Pour the batter into a greased 9x13 inch baking dish. Bake for 25-30 minutes or until a toothpick inserted in the center comes out clean.
While the cake is baking, prepare the cream cheese frosting. In a large mixing bowl, beat cream cheese and butter together until smooth. Gradually add powdered sugar and vanilla extract, mixing until smooth. Add milk as needed to thin out the frosting.
Once the cake has cooled, spread the cream cheese frosting over the top of the cake. Top with the reserved roasted strawberries.
This roasted strawberry sheet cake is perfect for any occasion, from birthday parties to summer picnics. The roasted strawberries add a rich, sweet flavor to the cake, and the tangy cream cheese frosting perfectly complements it. Enjoy!

Baileys Cheesecake

Ingredients
Cookie Crust

cooking spray
20 java chip flavored creme chocolate sandwich cookies (such as
Oreo)
2 tablespoons butter, melted

Cheesecake Filling
3 (8 ounce) packages cream cheese, at room temperature
3/4 cup sour cream, at room temperature
3/4 cup granulated sugar
1 tablespoon instant espresso powder
1 teaspoon vanilla extract
1/4 teaspoon salt
3 large eggs, at room temperature
1/2 cup Irish cream liqueur (such as Baileys)

Baileys Ganache

1/4 cup heavy cream
1/4 cup Irish cream liqueur (such as Baileys)
1 teaspoon instant espresso powder
1 cup milk chocolate chips
sweetened whipped cream for serving

Preheat the oven to 350 degrees F (175 degrees C) with rack in lower third position. Lightly grease an 8-inch springform pan with cooking spray
and line with parchment on the bottom.
Process cookies in a food processor until ground into small crumbs, 2 to 3 minutes. Pour in melted butter and process for another 30 seconds.
Press evenly into bottom and about 1 inch up sides of prepared pan.
Bake in the preheated oven until firm and fragrant, 10 to 12 minutes. Let cool slightly while making the filling, about 10 minutes.
Reduce oven temperature to 300 degrees F (150 degrees C).
Once crust is cooled, wrap bottom of pan with 2 layers of heavy-duty aluminum foil to prevent water from seeping into pan.
To make the cheesecake filling: Add cream cheese to the bowl of a stand mixer fitted with the paddle attachment and beat on medium-low
speed until creamy, about 2 minutes. Add sour cream, and beat on medium-low speed until fully combined, scraping down sides of bowl
halfway through, about 2 minutes.
Beat in sugar, espresso powder, vanilla, and salt, until combined, scraping down the sides of the bowl halfway through, about 1 minute. Add eggs,
1 at a time, beating on low speed just until combined after each addition and scraping down sides of bowl with a rubber spatula, 1 to 2 minutes.
Rest of ingredients added to sour cream and cream cheese mixture, beaten until well combined.
Add Baileys and beat on low speed until just combined, about 45 seconds.
Pour filling onto cooled crust. Place springform pan into a larger roasting pan and place in preheated oven. Pour 1 1/2 cups of water in roasting
pan and bake until the cheesecake is almost set (the center 2 inches should jiggle slightly) and edges have pulled away slightly from pan, 50 to 60
minutes.
Filling poured into crust and placed on a baking pan with water.
Turn off oven and leave door cracked open about 7 to 8 inches; let cheesecake stand in oven 30 minutes. Remove from oven and carefully lift
cheesecake from water bath. Cover and chill at least 3 hours or overnight.
Cheesecake removed from water bath and cooling.
To make the ganache: Heat cream and Baileys in a small saucepan over medium heat until warm to the touch, 3 to 4 minutes. Stir in espresso
powder until fully combined. Add chocolate chips and let stand 1 minute; stir until smooth.
Ganache ingredients combined in a sauce pan.
Remove cheesecake from pan and place on a cake plate. Pour ganache evenly over chilled cheesecake, spreading slightly over edges with an
offset spatula. Refrigerate until ganache is firm, about 30 minutes.

Neapolitan Nesquik Layer Cake

Ingredients
Cake:

2 cups white sugar
1 ½ cups unsalted butter, at room temperature
6 eggs, at room temperature, separated
1 ½ teaspoons vanilla extract
3 ½ cups unbleached all-purpose flour
4 ½ teaspoons baking powder
2 pinches salt, divided
1 ½ cups whole milk, at room temperature
½ cup chocolate-flavored milk powder (such as Nesquik®)
½ cup strawberry-flavored milk powder (such as Nesquik®)
9 drops red food coloring, or as desired

Cream Cheese Frosting:

1 (8 ounce) package cream cheese, at room temperature
½ cup unsalted butter, at room temperature
½ cup shortening
1 (16 ounce) package confectioners' sugar

Preheat the oven to 350 degrees F (175 degrees C). Grease and flour three 9-inch round cake pans.

Combine sugar and butter in a bowl and cream using an electric mixer until light and fluffy, scraping down the sides and blending for a total of 5 minutes. Add egg yolks slowly, 1 at a time, beating into creamed butter mixture. Beat in vanilla extract.

Sift flour, baking powder, and 1 pinch salt together in a separate bowl. Add to creamed sugar mixture in 3 batches, alternating with milk and blending after each addition. Scrape down the sides and bottom of the bowl and blend for 1 minute more; batter should be smooth and consistent. Separate batter evenly into 3 mixing bowls, about 2 1/2 cups in each.

Beat egg whites and remaining salt together in a bowl using a whip attachment until stiff peaks form.

Fold 1/3 of the whipped egg whites into 1 bowl of batter and pour into a prepared cake pan for the vanilla layer.

Fold 1/3 of the whipped egg whites and chocolate-flavored milk powder into another bowl of batter. Pour into another prepared cake pan for the chocolate layer.

Fold remaining 1/3 of the whipped egg whites, strawberry-flavored milk powder, and red food coloring into remaining bowl of batter. Pour into the remaining prepared cake pan for the strawberry layer.

Bake cake layers in the preheated oven until a toothpick inserted into the center of each comes out clean, 25 to 30 minutes. Remove from the oven and cool for about 15 minutes before flipping layers onto a wire rack to cool to room temperature, 20 to 30 minutes more.

Combine cream cheese, butter, and shortening in a bowl and cream together until smooth. Scrape down the bowl and add confectioners' sugar. Blend until frosting is smooth.

Assemble and frost the cooled cake layers and decorate as you please.

Zucchini Cake

Ingredients
Cake:

3 cups all-purpose flour
3 cups white sugar
2 ½ teaspoons ground cinnamon
1 ½ teaspoons baking soda
1 teaspoon baking powder
1 teaspoon salt
1 ½ cups vegetable oil
4 eggs
1 teaspoon vanilla extract
3 cups grated zucchini

Frosting:

1 (8 ounce) package cream cheese, room
temperature
½ cup butter, room temperature
2 cups confectioners' sugar, sifted
2 teaspoons vanilla extract

Preheat the oven to 325 degrees F (165 degrees C). Lightly grease and flour three 9-inch round cake pans.

Make the cake: Whisk flour, sugar, cinnamon, baking soda, baking powder, and salt together in a bowl until well combined.

Beat oil, eggs, and vanilla in a separate bowl with an electric mixer; pour into flour mixture and stir until well combined. Stir in shredded zucchini. Pour batter into the prepared pans.

Bake in the preheated oven until a tester inserted into each layer comes out clean, about 25 minutes. Remove from the oven and cool in the pans for 10 minutes, then invert layers onto a wire rack and let cool completely, 20 to 30 more minutes.

While the layers are cooling, make the frosting: Beat cream cheese and butter in a mixing bowl with an electric mixer until smooth. Mix in confectioner's sugar, a little at a time, until smooth. Stir in vanilla.

Place one cooled cake layer onto a serving plate. Cover with frosting and spread to the edges. Repeat with a second layer. Place remaining cake layer on top. Frost the sides of the cake, then finish by frosting the top.

Marble Cake

Ingredients
2 cups all-purpose flour
1 cup white sugar
1 cup milk
2 large eggs
½ cup butter, softened
2 teaspoons baking powder
1 teaspoon vanilla extract
½ teaspoon salt
2 tablespoons unsweetened cocoa powder

Preheat the oven to 350 degrees F (175 degrees C). Grease and flour a 9-inch round pan.
Place flour, sugar, milk, eggs, butter, baking powder, vanilla, and salt into a large bowl.
Batter ingredients placed in a large bowl.
Mix slowly to moisten, then beat with an electric mixer at medium speed for about 2 minutes until smooth.
Ingredients mixed together until smooth.
Reserve 3/4 cup batter; pour remaining batter into the prepared pan.
Batter poured into prepared pan, and some reserved in a small bowl.
Stir cocoa into reserved batter until even in color.
Cocoa stirred into reserved batter.
Drop chocolate batter by large spoonful on top of vanilla batter; swirl cocoa batter into white batter using a knife to create a marbled appearance.
Cocoa batter dropped into pan, and stirred to create a marbled appearance.
Bake in the preheated oven until a toothpick inserted into the center comes out clean, about 30 to 35 minutes. Cool briefly on a wire rack before inverting carefully onto a serving plate or cooling rack. Let cool completely.

Baked marble cake cooling on a cooling rack.

Chocolate Ganache Cake

Ingredients
FOR THE CAKE
Nonstick baking spray
3/4 c. all-purpose flour
1 c. granulated sugar
1/3 c. unsweetened cocoa powder
1 tsp. baking soda
1/2 tsp. baking powder
3/4 tsp. salt
1/2 c. buttermilk
1/4 c. canola oil
1 large egg, at room temperature
1 1/2 tsp. vanilla extract
1/2 c. freshly brewed strong coffee
FOR THE CHOCOLATE GANACHE
1 c. bittersweet chocolate chips
1 tbsp. salted butter
1 c. heavy cream
1 1/2 tbsp. light corn syrup
FOR THE PEANUT BUTTER GANACHE SWIRL (OPTIONAL)
1/2 c. peanut butter chips
1 tbsp. salted butter

Preheat the oven to 350°. Spray a 9-inch round cake pan with nonstick baking spray. Line the bottom of the pan with parchment paper and spray with nonstick baking spray. Set the pan aside.

Sift the flour, sugar, cocoa powder, baking soda, baking powder, and salt in a large bowl; whisk to combine. In a separate large bowl, whisk together the buttermilk, oil, egg and vanilla. Gradually add the flour mixture to the buttermilk mixture, and whisk until well combined. Add the coffee and whisk just until evenly incorporated.

Transfer the batter to the prepared pan and bake for 28 to 32 minutes, until a toothpick comes out clean. Let the cake cool in the pan for 15 minutes. Invert onto a cooling rack to cool completely, 1 hour.

For the chocolate ganache: In a 4-cup heat-proof liquid measuring cup with a spout, combine the chocolate chips and 1 tablespoon butter. In a small saucepan, bring the cream and light corn syrup to low simmer over medium-low heat. Pour the cream mixture over the chocolate mixture and let it stand for 2 minutes. Stir until very smooth. Set aside until cooled slightly, but still pourable (about 105°), 2 to 5 minutes.

While chocolate ganache is cooling, set the cake, still on the wire rack, in a rimmed baking sheet.

Once the ganache has cooled slightly, pour it over the cake, making sure to completely cover the top and sides, letting any excess run off into the rimmed baking sheet. Smooth the top of the cake using a large offset spatula. Immediately transfer the cake to the refrigerator to harden the ganache, 30 minutes. Using 2 large spatulas, carefully transfer the cake to a serving platter. Serve slightly chilled or at room temperature.8For the peanut butter ganache swirl (optional): While the chocolate ganache is cooling in Step 4, combine the peanut butter chips and butter in a small microwavable bowl. Microwave on high until mixture is melted and smooth, 30 seconds, stopping to stir after 15 seconds. Transfer peanut butter mixture to a small Ziploc bag with a 1/4-inch hole cut in the corner. Immediately after covering the cake with warm ganache in Step 6, pipe 6 equally spaced lines of the peanut butter mixture across the top of the cake. Using a paring knife or skewer, drag the tip through the peanut butter and ganache in 7 evenly spaced lines perpendicular to the piped peanut butter, alternating the direction of each line. Proceed with Step 7 and cool cake as directed.

Coconut Layer Cake

Ingredients
FOR THE CAKE:
3 sticks unsalted butter, at room temperature, plus
more for the pans
1 1/2 c. all-purpose flour, plus more for the pans
2 3/4 c. cake flour (not self-rising)
1 tbsp. plus 1/4 teaspoon baking powder
1 1/4 tsp. kosher salt
2 1/4 c. sugar
3 large eggs, plus 3 egg whites
1 tbsp. coconut extract
1 tsp. vanilla extract
1 1/2 c. whole milk
FOR THE FROSTING:
2 c. sugar
8 large egg whites
6 sticks unsalted butter, cut into pieces, at room
temperature
1 tbsp. coconut extract
1 tsp. vanilla extract
Pinch of kosher salt
2 c. sweetened shredded coconut

Directions

Make the cake: Preheat the oven to 350°. Butter three 8-inch round cake pans and line the bottoms with parchment, then butter the parchment. Dust with all-purpose flour and tap out the excess. Whisk the all-purpose flour, cake flour, baking powder and salt in a medium bowl. Set aside.

Beat the butter and sugar in a large bowl with a mixer on medium speed until pale and fluffy, 3 to 5 minutes. Add the eggs and egg whites one at a time, beating well after each addition and scraping down the bowl as necessary. Beat in both extracts. Reduce the mixer speed to low and gradually beat in the flour mixture in three batches, alternating with the milk. Beat until just incorporated.

Divide the batter evenly among the prepared pans. Bake until the cakes are golden around the edges and a toothpick inserted into the centers comes out clean, 40 to 45 minutes. Transfer to racks and let the cakes cool in the pans for 15 minutes. Remove the cakes from the pans, remove the parchment and return the cakes to the racks to cool completely.

While the cakes cool, make the frosting: Combine the sugar and egg whites in a heatproof bowl set over a pan of simmering water (do not let the bowl touch the water). Whisk until warm and the sugar is dissolved, 3 to 4 minutes. Remove the bowl from the pan and beat with a mixer on medium speed until thick and glossy, 5 minutes. Increase the speed to medium high and beat until stiff peaks form and the bottom of the bowl is cool, 7 more minutes. Reduce the speed to medium low. Add the butter a few tablespoons at a time, beating well after each addition. (It's OK if the frosting looks separated—just beat on medium-high speed until smooth again.) Add both extracts and the salt and continue beating until fluffy, 3 to 5 minutes.

Trim the tops of the cakes with a long serrated knife to make them level, if necessary. Place 1 cake layer on a cake stand or platter. Spread with 1 cup frosting. Place the second layer on top and spread with another 1 cup frosting. Place the remaining cake layer on top and spread the remaining frosting over the top and sides of the cake. Press the coconut into the sides of the cake.

Apple Cake

Ingredients

Non-stick baking spray (with flour)
2/3 c. light brown sugar
2 large eggs
1/3 c. apple butter
1/4 c. unsalted butter, melted
1 1/2 tsp. vanilla extract
1 1/4 c. all-purpose flour
1 1/2 tsp. baking powder
1 tsp. cinnamon
3/4 tsp. kosher salt
1/2 tsp. baking soda
2 small Granny Smith apples, peeled and
chopped (about 2 cups chopped)
1/2 c. chopped toasted pecans
Powdered sugar, for dusting

Preheat the oven to 350°F. Prepare a 9-inch round baking pan with non-stick baking spray and line the bottom of the pan with parchment paper.

In a large bowl, whisk together the sugar, eggs, apple butter, melted butter and vanilla until well combined. Add the flour, baking powder, cinnamon, salt and baking soda. Whisk until just combined. Add the apples and pecans and fold in with a rubber spatula to incorporate. Transfer the batter to the prepared pan and spread in an even layer. Bake until a toothpick comes out clean, 28 to 32 minutes.

Remove the cake from the oven and cool in the pan for 10 minutes. Remove the cake from the pan, remove and discard the parchment paper and place cake on a wire rack to cool completely, about 1 hour.

Dust the cake lightly with powdered sugar just before serving.

Gingerbread Cake

Ingredients
FOR THE CAKE:
2 1/2 c. all-purpose flour
2 tsp. baking powder
2 tsp. ground ginger
1 tsp. ground cinnamon
1/2 tsp. ground cloves
1/2 tsp. salt
1/4 tsp. baking soda
1 c. unsulphured molasses
1 c. hot water
3/4 c. granulated sugar
1 stick butter, melted
2 large eggs
2 tsp. vanilla extract
Nonstick spray baking spray with flour
FOR THE FROSTING
8 oz. cream cheese, softened
2 sticks unsalted butter, softened
5 c. powdered sugar
2 tsp. grated lemon zest (from 1 lemon)
Chopped candied ginger, optional
White or gold sparkling sugar, optional

Preheat the oven to 350F.

For the cake: In a large bowl, whisk together the flour, baking powder, ginger, cinnamon, cloves, salt, and baking soda.

In a medium bowl, stir together the molasses and hot water until fully combined. Whisk in the butter, sugar, eggs, and vanilla until smooth. Pour the wet mixture into dry mixture and whisk just until no dry streaks are left (do not over mix).

Spray a 13x9-inch cake pan with baking spray (or grease with butter). Pour the batter into the prepared pan. Bake for 25 to 30 minutes or until a toothpick inserted into the center comes out with a few moist crumbs. Let cool completely in the pan on a wire rack.

For the frosting: Combine the cream cheese and butter in a large bowl. Beat with a hand mixer (or use a stand mixer with a paddle attachment) until fully combined, about 1 minute. Gradually add the powdered sugar and beat until combined. Beat in the lemon zest and continue beating until light and fluffy, 1 more minute. Spread the frosting over the cooled cake. Garnish with candied ginger and gold sparkling sugar, if desired.

Vegan Chocolate Cake

Ingredients:

For the cake:

1 1/2 cups all-purpose flour
1 cup granulated sugar
1/2 cup unsweetened cocoa
powder 1 tsp baking soda
1/2 tsp salt
1 cup unsweetened almond milk
1/2 cup vegetable oil
2 tbsp apple cider vinegar
2 tsp vanilla extract

For the frosting:

1/2 cup vegan butter, softened
2 cups powdered sugar
1/4 cup unsweetened cocoa powder 1 tsp vanilla
extract
2-3 tbsp unsweetened almond milk

Instructions:

Preheat your oven to 350°F (180°C). Grease a 9-inch round cake pan with cooking spray.
In a mixing bowl, whisk together the all-purpose flour, granulated sugar, unsweetened cocoa powder,
baking soda, and salt.
In a separate bowl, mix together the unsweetened almond milk, vegetable oil, apple cider vinegar,
and vanilla extract.
Gradually stir the wet ingredients into the dry ingredients until well combined and the batter is
smooth. Pour the batter into the prepared cake pan and smooth the surface with a spatula.
Bake for 30-35 minutes or until a toothpick inserted into the center of the cake comes out clean.
Allow the cake to cool in the pan for 10 minutes before transferring it to a wire rack to cool
completely. To make the frosting, beat the softened vegan butter with an electric mixer until light
and fluffy. Gradually beat in the powdered sugar, unsweetened cocoa powder, and vanilla extract
until well combined.
Add in the unsweetened almond milk, one tablespoon at a time, until the frosting is smooth and
spreadable.
Once the cake is completely cooled, spread the frosting evenly over the top and sides of the cake.
Enjoy your delicious vegan chocolate cake!

Cherry Chocolate Marble Cake

Ingredients:

For the Cake:

2 cups all-purpose flour
2 teaspoons baking powder
1/4 teaspoon baking soda
1/2 teaspoon salt
1/2 cup unsalted butter, room temperature 1 cup
granulated sugar
2 large eggs
1/2 cup whole milk
1/2 cup cherry juice
1 teaspoon vanilla extract
1/2 cup chocolate chips
For the Cherry Swirl:
1 cup frozen cherries, pitted and chopped 1/4 cup
granulated sugar

Instructions:

Preheat the oven to 350°F. Grease and flour a 9x5-inch loaf pan.
In a medium bowl, whisk together the flour, baking powder, baking soda, and salt.
In a large mixing bowl, cream the butter and sugar together until light and fluffy.
Add the eggs one at a time, mixing well after each addition.
Add half of the dry ingredients to the mixing bowl and mix until just combined.
Add the milk, cherry juice, and vanilla extract to the mixing bowl and mix until combined.
Add the remaining dry ingredients to the mixing bowl and mix until just combined.
Melt the chocolate chips in the microwave or over a double boiler and add them to the mixing bowl.
Mix until combined.
In a separate bowl, mix together the chopped cherries and sugar.
Pour half of the cake batter into the prepared loaf pan.
Add spoonfuls of the cherry mixture over the cake batter.
Pour the remaining cake batter over the cherry mixture.
Use a butter knife or toothpick to swirl the cherry mixture into the cake batter.
Bake for 50-60 minutes, or until a toothpick inserted into the center of the cake comes out clean.
Allow the cake to cool in the pan for 10 minutes before transferring it to a wire rack to cool completely.
Slice your Cherry Chocolate Marble Cake and serve it with a cup of coffee or tea for a delightful and decadent treat!

Pumpkin Spice Cake

Ingredients
FOR THE CAKE
2 1/2 c. granulated sugar
1 c. vegetable oil
3 large eggs
3 c. all-purpose flour
2 tsp. baking soda
1 tsp. ground cinnamon
1 1/2 tsp. pumpkin pie spice
1/2 tsp. salt
1 15 oz. can pumpkin puree
1/2 tsp. vanilla extract
Nonstick cooking spray with flour
FOR THE CARAMEL GLAZE:
1 14 oz. can sweetened condensed milk
1 c. packed light brown sugar
2 tbsp. salted butter
1/4 tsp. vanilla extract

Preheat oven to 350°.
Add the sugar and oil to the bowl of a stand-up mixture with a paddle attachment. Beat on medium speed until well mixed. Add the eggs, one at a time, beating well after each addition. Mix in the vanilla.

In a medium bowl, combine the flour, baking soda, cinnamon, pumpkin pie spice, and salt. Add one-third of the flour mixture to the wet mixture, then mix to combine. Add one-half of the pumpkin puree, then mix to combine. Repeat with the flour mixture, more pumpkin, then finishing with flour, mixing well between each addition until the batter is smooth.

Spray the inside of a 12-cup bundt pan with non-stick baking spray with flour, then pour the batter into the pan. Place a folded kitchen towel on the counter and tap the pan (use some force!) on the towel 8-10 times (to remove any air bubbles in the batter). Bake 60 to 65 minutes or until a wooden pick inserted into the center comes out clean. Let cool in the pan for 10 minutes then place a wire cooling rack over the pan and flip to remove the cake. Let cool completely.

For the Caramel Glaze: In a medium saucepan, add the milk and sugar and cook over medium-low heat until it comes to a boil, stirring constantly. Reduce the heat to low and simmer for 8 minutes, stirring frequently. Remove from the heat and strain through a fine mesh strainer. Stir in the butter and vanilla. Let cool for 10-12 minutes, stirring frequently. The icing is ready when it makes thick ribbons when drizzled (it will still be warm). Drizzle it all over the cake. Let the glaze cool completely before cutting.

Sponge Cake

Ingredients

CAKE

2 large eggs, room temperature
1 cup (200 g) granulated sugar
2 tsp. vanilla bean paste or vanilla extract
1 tsp. Diamond Crystal or ½ tsp. Morton kosher salt
1 tsp. baking powder
1 cup (125 g) bleached all-purpose flour
½ cup whole milk
6 Tbsp. unsalted butter, cut into 1" pieces

FILLING AND ASSEMBLY

⅓ cup raspberry or strawberry jam
2 tsp. fresh lemon juice
¾ tsp. Diamond Crystal or ½ tsp. Morton kosher salt, divided
1 cup heavy cream
1 Tbsp. plus 2 tsp. granulated sugar
1 Tbsp. instant vanilla pudding mix
1 tsp. vanilla bean paste or vanilla extract
Powdered sugar (for dusting)

Preparation

CAKE

Place a rack in middle of oven; preheat to 350°. Line two 8"-diameter cake pans with parchment paper rounds (do not grease). Beat 2 large eggs, room temperature, 1 cup (200 g) granulated sugar, 2 tsp. vanilla bean paste or vanilla extract, and 1 tsp. Diamond Crystal or ½ tsp. Morton kosher salt in the bowl of a stand mixer fitted with the whisk attachment on medium speed until pale, fluffy, and nearly tripled in volume, 10–15 minutes (mixture will form an unbroken ribbon when whisk is lifted from bowl). Reduce speed to low, add 1 tsp. baking powder, and beat, scraping down sides of bowl halfway through, until well combined, about 1 minute. Add 1 cup (125 g) bleached all-purpose flour and beat until incorporated, about 1 minute (batter will be very thick); scrape down sides and bottom of bowl.

Meanwhile, heat ½ cup whole milk and 6 Tbsp. unsalted butter, cut into 1" pieces, in a small saucepan over medium, stirring occasionally with a heatproof rubber spatula, until butter is melted and milk is steaming (but nowhere near boiling), about 4 minutes. Pour milk mixture over batter, scraping saucepan to get every bit. Beat on low speed until combined and batter is smooth, about 2 minutes. Scrape down sides and bottom of bowl and fold gently once or twice to ensure batter is well combined (it will be runny).

Divide batter between prepared pans (about 325 g per pan). Bake cakes until golden brown and tops spring back when lightly pressed, 20–25 minutes. Transfer pans to a wire rack and let cakes cool 10 minutes. Run an offset spatula around sides of cakes to loosen, then invert onto rack; peel away parchment. Let cool completely, about 1 hour.

Do ahead: Cakes can be baked 1 day ahead. Store tightly wrapped at room temperature.

FILLING AND ASSEMBLY

Stir together ⅓ cup raspberry or strawberry jam, 2 tsp. fresh lemon juice, and ¼ tsp. Diamond Crystal or Morton kosher salt in a small bowl.

Whip 1 cup heavy cream, 1 Tbsp. plus 2 tsp. granulated sugar, 1 Tbsp. instant vanilla pudding mix, 1 tsp. vanilla bean paste or vanilla extract, and remaining ½ tsp. Diamond Crystal or ¼ tsp. Morton kosher salt in the clean bowl of a stand mixer fitted with the whisk attachment on medium speed until medium-firm peaks form (it's okay if there are tiny lumps of pudding mix; they'll be imperceptible), about 4 minutes. Scrape down sides and bottom of bowl and fold gently to ensure mixture is uniform.

Place 1 cake layer, right side up, on a cake stand or large plate. Spread jam mixture over top, leaving a ¼" border around the edges. Dollop whipped cream over and spread evenly all the way to the edges with an offset spatula. Place second cake layer, upside down, on top and press gently to adhere. Dust lightly with powdered sugar.

To serve, slice cake into wedges with a serrated knife, wiping clean between cuts.

Do ahead: Cake (without powdered sugar) can be assembled 1 day ahead. Cover loosely and chill. Bring to room temperature before serving.

Chocolate Lava Cake

Ingredients

¼ cup heavy cream
7 ounces bittersweet chocolate, chopped into small pieces, divided
6 tablespoons unsalted butter, plus more for ramekins
Demerara or raw sugar (for sprinkling)
3 large eggs
⅓ cup light brown sugar
1 teaspoon vanilla extract
3 tablespoons all-purpose flour
½ teaspoon kosher salt
SPECIAL EQUIPMENT
Four 6-ounce ramekins

Heat cream in a small saucepan over medium until just beginning to simmer. Place 2 oz. chocolate in a small bowl; pour hot cream over. Stir until smooth. Chill ganache until firm, at least 1 hour.

Preheat oven to 425°. Coat ramekins with butter and sprinkle with demerara sugar, tapping out excess.

Combine 6 Tbsp. butter and remaining 5 oz. chocolate in a medium heatproof bowl set over a large saucepan of barely simmering water (do not let water touch bowl); stir constantly until chocolate is melted (you can also do this step in the microwave).

Using an electric mixer on medium-high speed, beat eggs and brown sugar in a large bowl until light and tripled in volume, about 4 minutes. Beat in vanilla.

Gently fold melted chocolate into egg mixture until incorporated. Fold in flour and salt until smooth.

Divide half of batter among prepared ramekins (about ⅓ cup each). Place 1 mounded Tbsp. ganache in the center of each partially filled ramekin. Divide remaining batter among ramekins.

Bake until tops are firm but cakes wobble slightly when jiggled, 13–15 minutes. Let cool 30 seconds before inverting onto small plates. Serve immediately.

Do Ahead: Ganache can be made 1 week ahead. Tightly wrap and keep chilled. Cakes can be assembled 1 week ahead. Tightly wrap with plastic in ramekins and freeze. Let sit at room temperature 1 hour before baking.

Raspberry Cake

Ingredients

CAKE
4 large eggs, room temperature, separated
1 tsp. Diamond Crystal or ½ tsp. Morton kosher salt
½ tsp. cream of tartar
1 cup (200 g) sugar, divided
⅓ cup vegetable oil
1 tsp. vanilla extract
1 cup (125 g) cake flour
½ tsp. baking powder

ASSEMBLY
1 cup (200 g) sugar
1½ cups (37 g) freeze-dried raspberries; plus more crushed for serving (optional)
3 cups heavy cream
1 tsp. vanilla extract
1 tsp. Diamond Crystal or ½ tsp. Morton kosher salt
¼ cup (80 g) raspberry jam
2 cups (170 g) fresh raspberries
SPECIAL EQUIPMENT
A pastry bag and a ½"-diameter tip

CAKE

die of oven: preheat to 350°. Line two 8"-diameter cake pans with parchment paper rounds (do not grease). Beat egg whites, salt, cream of tartar, and ½ cup (100 g) sugar in the bowl of a stand mixer fitted with the whisk attachment on medium-low speed until egg whites are broken up, about 30 seconds. Increase speed to medium-high and beat until meringue is glossy and holds firm peaks, 8–10 minutes.

Whisk egg yolks and remaining ½ cup (100 g) sugar by hand in a large bowl until pale and well combined, about 2 minutes. Whisk in oil, vanilla, and ⅓ cup room-temperature water. Sift flour and baking powder over and whisk vigorously to combine.

Add one fourth of meringue to egg yolk mixture and mix thoroughly to incorporate (this will lighten the batter). Add remaining meringue in 3 batches, gently folding after each addition until only a few streaks of meringue remain (err on the side of mixing slightly less rather than more to keep batter billowy).

Divide batter evenly between prepared pans and gently smooth surface. Bake cakes 15 minutes. Reduce oven temperature to 325° and continue baking until golden brown and tops spring back when gently pressed, 35–40 minutes more. Remove from oven; invert pans onto a wire rack. Let cakes cool in pans (cooling them upside down reduces shrinkage), 60–70 minutes. Turn cakes over and run an offset spatula around sides of cakes to loosen, then invert cakes onto wire rack. Peel away parchment.

ASSEMBLY

Finely grind sugar and 1½ cups (37 g) freeze-dried raspberries in a spice mill or food processor (if using food processor, sift powder through a fine-mesh sieve after to remove seeds). Transfer to the clean bowl of a stand mixer fitted with the whisk attachment; add cream, vanilla, and salt and beat on medium-high speed until firm peaks form, 5–7 minutes.

Stir jam in a small bowl to loosen, then gently fold in fresh raspberries.

Place 1 cake on a cake platter or large plate. Scoop a heaping cupful of raspberry cream on top; spread evenly with offset spatula. Spoon berry mixture on top of cream, leaving a 1" border around the edges (this will prevent berries from spilling over the sides). Place second cake layer on top. Spoon a heaping ½ cup raspberry cream into pastry bag fitted with tip. Frost top and sides of cake with raspberry cream still in bowl, then pipe dollops of raspberry cream around edges of top of cake. Chill cake, uncovered, at least 2 hours.

To serve, sprinkle top of cake with crushed freeze-dried raspberries if desired. Slice cake with a serrated knife, wiping clean between cuts.

Do ahead: Cake can be baked 1 day ahead; store tightly wrapped at room temperature, or freeze up to 1 week. If frozen, thaw in refrigerator overnight before using. Cake (without crushed raspberry topping) can be assembled 1 day ahead; cover loosely and chill.

Lemon Tea Cake

Ingredients
Makes one 8½x4½" loaf

½ cup extra-virgin olive oil, plus more for parchment
1 preserved lemon (about 55 g)
1½ cups (188 g) all purpose flour
2 tsp. baking powder
½ tsp. ground turmeric
3 large eggs
1 cup plus 2 Tbsp. (225 g) granulated sugar
½ cup sour cream
1 Tbsp. finely grated lemon zest
3 Tbsp. fresh lemon juice
¾ cup (83 g) powdered sugar
1 Tbsp. whole milk

Flaky sea salt

Place a rack in middle of oven; preheat to 350°. Line an 8½x4½" loaf pan, preferably metal, with parchment paper, leaving generous overhang on the long sides, and brush with oil. Cut preserved lemon into quarters; remove any seeds. Transfer to a small food processor and process to form a paste (you can also do this with a mortar and pestle or simply chop and smash with your knife).

Whisk flour, baking powder, and turmeric in a medium bowl to combine. Beat eggs, granulated sugar, and remaining ½ cup oil in the bowl of a stand mixer fitted with the paddle attachment on medium speed until smooth and incorporated, about 1 minute. Add sour cream and mix to combine. Add preserved-lemon paste, lemon zest, and lemon juice and mix to combine. Reduce speed to low, add dry ingredients, and mix until just combined, about 15 seconds. (Batter can also be mixed together in a large bowl with a whisk.) Scrape batter into prepared pan and smooth top.

Bake cake until top is golden brown and a tester inserted into the center comes out clean, 50–60 minutes. Transfer pan to a wire rack and let cake cool 15 minutes. Run a knife around sides of pan to loosen and, using parchment paper overhang, lift cake out of pan and onto rack. Peel away parchment paper and discard. Let cake cool completely.

Meanwhile, whisk powdered sugar and milk in a medium bowl until smooth.

Transfer cake to a platter or large plate. Using a rubber spatula to help guide glaze, spoon glaze over cake, letting it drip down the sides (you should have a fairly thick coating). Sprinkle sea salt over glaze and let cake sit until glaze is set, about 30 minutes.

Do ahead: Cake can be made 3 days ahead. Store airtight at room temperature.

Cake With Mascarpone

Ingredients
12 servings
SOAK
¾cup (190 g) sweet Marsala
½cup plus 2 Tbsp. (150 g) brewed espresso, cooled
FILLING
1½tsp. unflavored powdered gelatin
1cup (224 g) heavy cream
4(59 g) large egg yolks, room temperature
2Tbsp. (26 g) sweet Marsala
2Tbsp. (26 g) granulated sugar
1tsp. vanilla extract
½tsp. kosher salt
8oz. (227 g) mascarpone
ASSEMBLY

<u>Vanilla Genoise</u>

<u>Espresso Swiss Meringue Buttercream</u>

SOAK
Combine Marsala and espresso in a small bowl. Cover and chill.

Do Ahead: Soak can be made 3 days ahead. Keep chilled.

FILLING
Place ¼ cup cold water in a small bowl and sprinkle gelatin evenly over top; chill until ready to use.

Beat cream in the bowl of a stand mixer fitted with the whisk attachment on medium-high speed until medium peaks form. Scrape whipped cream into a medium bowl; cover and chill. Reserve bowl; you don't need to clean it.

Whisk egg yolks, Marsala, sugar, vanilla, and salt in a medium heatproof bowl until smooth; set over a saucepan of just barely simmering water (do not let bowl touch water). Heat, whisking constantly, until yolks are lightened in color and doubled in volume, about 5 minutes. Mixture should feel warm to the touch. Remove egg yolk mixture from heat and scrape into reserved bowl. Fit bowl onto mixer.
Remove saucepan from heat and pour out water, then scrape in softened gelatin. Heat over medium-low, swirling pan often, until gelatin is dissolved, about 1 minute. With mixer on medium speed, stream gelatin into egg yolk mixture. Beat until sides of bowl are cool to the touch, about 2 minutes; add mascarpone and beat until smooth.
Remove bowl from mixer and gently fold in chilled whipped cream. You should have about 4 cups mousse. Cover with plastic wrap, pressing directly onto surface; chill until set, at least 4 hours.
Do Ahead: Mousse can be made 3 days ahead. Keep chilled.

ASSEMBLY
Line a 9"-diameter cake pan or springform pan with plastic wrap, pressing into bottom and leaving generous overhang. Fit a 1-piece round of cake into pan, placing bottom side up. Using a pastry brush, dab a quarter of soak across entire surface of cake. Stir chilled mousse to loosen, then scrape a third over cake and smooth into an even layer with a small offset spatula. Place another round of cake, bottom side up, on top of mousse, this time using a 2-piece layer. Repeat soaking and filling process. Top with the remaining 2-piece round of cake, bottom side up, and repeat soaking and filling process one more time. Top with remaining 1-piece round of cake, bottom side up, and brush with remaining soak. You should have 4 layers of soaked cake separated by 3 layers of filling. Wrap plastic overhang up and over cake; chill at least 12 hours and up to 2 days to allow mousse to set and cake to absorb soak.
To frost, remove plastic from top of cake and invert cake onto a cake plate or platter. Remove pan and plastic. Dollop about 1 cup buttercream over top of cake and smooth across top and down sides, creating a very thin base layer. You want to fill in any gaps, adhere any crumbs to the cake, and seal in the fillings (this is called a crumb coat). Chill cake 10 minutes, then scrape remaining frosting on top of cake and spread all over, working down and around sides. Decorate as desired.
Do Ahead: Cake can be made 2 days ahead. Chill until frosting sets, then cover loosely with plastic wrap. Let sit at room temperature 1–1½ hours before slicing.

Cinnamon Coffee Cake

For the Cinnamon Streusel:

1/2 cup brown sugar
1/2 cup all-purpose flour
1 tsp ground cinnamon
1/4 cup unsalted butter, melted and
cooled

Instructions:

Preheat the oven to 350°F. Grease a 9-inch springform pan with cooking spray.
In a large mixing bowl, whisk together the flour, sugar, baking powder, baking soda, and salt. In another bowl, whisk together the Greek yogurt, melted butter, eggs, and vanilla extract. Pour the wet ingredients into the dry ingredients and mix until just combined. In a small bowl, mix together the brown sugar, flour, and cinnamon for the cinnamon streusel. Pour half of the cake batter into the prepared springform pan.
Sprinkle half of the cinnamon streusel over the batter.
Pour the remaining cake batter on top of the cinnamon streusel.
Sprinkle the remaining cinnamon streusel on top of the cake batter.
Use a knife to gently swirl the cinnamon streusel into the batter.
Bake the cake for 40-45 minutes or until a toothpick inserted into the center comes out clean. Allow the cake to cool in the pan for 10-15 minutes.
Run a knife around the edges of the cake to loosen it from the pan.
Remove the sides of the springform pan and transfer the cake to a serving plate.
Slice and serve the Cinnamon Coffee Cake warm or at room temperature.
Enjoy your delicious and moist Cinnamon Coffee Cake with a cup of hot coffee or tea!

Cream Coffee Cake

Ingredients
10 servings

1 cup (2 sticks) unsalted butter, room temperature, plus more for pan
2 cups all-purpose flour, plus more for pan
1 Tbsp. baking powder
¼ tsp. kosher salt
1½ cups shelled pecans, coarsely chopped
1 Tbsp. ground cinnamon
2½ cups sugar, divided
2 large eggs, beaten to blend
2 cups sour cream
1 Tbsp. vanilla extract

Preparation

Place a rack in middle of oven; preheat to 350°. Butter and flour Bundt pan. Sift baking powder, salt, and 2 cups flour into a medium bowl.

Mix pecans, cinnamon, and ½ cup sugar in another medium bowl.

Using an electric mixer on medium-high speed, beat remaining 2 cups sugar and 1 cup butter in a large bowl until incorporated and smooth. Add eggs, beating well to combine and scraping down bowl, then beat in sour cream and vanilla.

Reduce mixer speed to low and beat flour mixture into butter mixture, increasing speed to medium-low if needed, until just blended. Do not overbeat. Scrape half of batter into prepared pan. Sprinkle evenly with half of pecan mixture. Spread remaining batter over; smooth top, then sprinkle with remaining pecan mixture.

Bake cake until a tester inserted into the center comes out clean, 50–55 minutes. Let cool 20–30 minutes. Invert onto a platter and serve warm.

Three-Layer Chocolate Ganache Cake

Ingredients for Cake Layers:

2 cups all-purpose flour
3/4 cup unsweetened cocoa powder 2 tsp
baking powder
1 tsp baking soda
1 tsp salt
2 cups granulated sugar
1 cup vegetable oil
4 large eggs
1 cup buttermilk
1 cup hot water
1 tsp vanilla extract
Ingredients for Chocolate Ganache:

8 oz semisweet chocolate, chopped 1 cup
heavy cream

Instructions:

Preheat your oven to 350°F. Grease three 8-inch round cake pans and line with parchment paper.
In a large bowl, sift together the flour, cocoa powder, baking powder, baking soda, and salt.
In another bowl, beat together the sugar and vegetable oil until well combined.
Add the eggs one at a time, beating well after each addition.
Mix in the buttermilk and vanilla extract.
Gradually add the dry ingredients to the wet ingredients, alternating with the hot water, and mix until smooth.
Divide the batter evenly among the prepared pans.
Bake for 25-30 minutes, or until a toothpick inserted in the center comes out clean.
Let the cake layers cool in the pans for 10 minutes before transferring to wire racks to cool completely.
While the cake layers cool, make the ganache. In a small saucepan, heat the heavy cream over medium heat until just simmering.
Remove from heat and pour the hot cream over the chopped chocolate. Stir until the chocolate is melted and smooth.
Let the ganache cool for about 30 minutes, until it thickens but is still spreadable.
To assemble the cake, place one cake layer on a serving plate or cake stand. Spread a layer of ganache on top of the cake. Repeat with the remaining cake layers and ganache, stacking the layers on top of each other.
Use the remaining ganache to frost the sides of the cake.
Refrigerate the cake for at least 30 minutes before serving.
Enjoy your delicious and decadent Three-Layer Chocolate Ganache Cake!

Vanilla Cake With Mango

Ingredients
12 servings
SOAK
½cup (100 g) sugar
Pinch of kosher salt
1vanilla bean, halved lengthwise
½cup (100 g) silver tequila
FILLING
1envelope unflavored powdered gelatin (about 2½ tsp.)
1(heaping) cup (200 g) fresh mango pieces (from 1 large
ripe mango), puréed until smooth
6Tbsp. (80 g) fresh lemon juice
1tsp. kosher salt
2cups (400 g) sugar, divided
3(150 g) large eggs
8(110 g) large egg yolks
6Tbsp. (85 g) chilled unsalted butter, cut into pieces
½cup (100 g) extra-virgin olive oil
ASSEMBLY
Vanilla Genoise
Vanilla Swiss Meringue Buttercream

Preparation
SOAK
Combine sugar, salt, and ½ cup water in a small saucepan; scrape in seeds from vanilla bean and discard pod. Bring to a simmer and cook 2 minutes.
Remove from heat and immediately pour in tequila. Strain into a small bowl (you should have about 1 cup). Cover and chill.
Do Ahead: Soak can be made 3 days ahead. Keep chilled.

FILLING

Place ½ cup cold water in a small bowl and sprinkle gelatin evenly over top; chill until ready to use.
Cook mango purée, lemon juice, salt, and 1½ cups sugar in a medium saucepan over medium-low, stirring to dissolve sugar, until steaming (don't boil), 5–
7 minutes.
Meanwhile, whisk eggs, egg yolks, and remaining ½ cup sugar in a medium bowl until pale and foamy, about 1 minute.
Ladle some mango mixture into egg mixture, whisking to combine, then stream egg mixture into remaining mango mixture, whisking constantly. Cook,
adjusting heat to keep mixture just under a simmer and stirring constantly with a heatproof rubber spatula, until thick enough to coat spatula and an
instant-read thermometer registers 170°, 8–10 minutes. Remove from heat and scrape in softened gelatin; stir to dissolve. Add butter, whisking in a piece
at a time, then gradually stream in oil, whisking constantly. Strain curd through a fine-mesh sieve into a medium bowl. Set in a larger bowl partially
filled with ice water and stir to cool quickly. You should have about 4½ cups curd. Remove from water and cover with plastic wrap, pressing directly
onto surface; chill until set, at least 4 hours.
Do Ahead: Curd can be made 3 days ahead. Keep chilled.

ASSEMBLY

Line a 9"-diameter cake pan or springform pan with plastic wrap, pressing into bottom and leaving generous overhang. Fit a 1-piece round of cake into
pan, placing bottom side up. Using a pastry brush, dab a quarter of soak across entire surface of cake. Stir chilled mango curd to loosen, then scrape a
third over cake and smooth in an even layer with a small offset spatula. Place another round of cake on top of curd, bottom side up, this time using a 2-
piece layer. Repeat soaking and filling process. Top with the remaining 2-piece round of cake, bottom side up, and repeat soaking and filling process
one more time. Top with remaining 1-piece round of cake, bottom side up, and brush with remaining soak. You should have 4 layers of soaked cake
separated by 3 layers of filling. Wrap plastic overhang up and over cake; chill at least 12 hours and up to 2 days to allow mango curd to set and cake to
absorb soak.

To frost, remove plastic from top of cake and invert cake onto a cake plate or platter. Remove pan and plastic. Dollop about 1 cup buttercream over top
of cake and smooth across top and down sides, creating a very thin layer. You want to fill in any gaps, adhere any crumbs to the cake, and seal in the
fillings (this is called a crumb coat). Chill cake 10 minutes, then scrape remaining frosting on top of cake and spread all over, working down and around
sides. Decorate as desired.

Do Ahead: Cake can be made 2 days ahead. Chill until frosting sets, then cover loosely with plastic wrap. Let sit at room temperature 1–1½ hours before
slicing.

Basque Burnt Cheesecake

Ingredients

Unsalted butter (for pan)
2lb. cream cheese, room temperature
1½cups sugar
6large eggs
2cups heavy cream
1tsp. kosher salt
1tsp. vanilla extract
⅓cup all-purpose flour
Sherry (for serving; optional)

Preparation

Place a rack in middle of oven; preheat to 400°. Butter pan, then line with 2 overlapping 16x12" sheets of parchment, making sure parchment comes at least 2" above top of pan on all sides. Because the parchment needs to be pleated and creased in some areas to fit in pan, you won't end up with a clean, smooth outer edge to the cake; that's okay! Place pan on a rimmed baking sheet.

Beat cream cheese and sugar in the bowl of a stand mixer fitted with the paddle attachment on medium-low speed, scraping down sides of bowl, until very smooth, no lumps remain, and sugar has dissolved, about 2 minutes.

Increase speed to medium and add eggs one at a time, beating each egg 15 seconds before adding the next. Scrape down sides of bowl, then reduce mixer speed to medium-low. Add cream, salt, and vanilla and beat until combined, about 30 seconds.

Turn off mixer and sift flour evenly over cream cheese mixture using a fine-mesh sieve. Beat on low speed until incorporated, about 15 seconds. Scrape down sides of bowl (yet again) and continue to beat until batter is very smooth, homogenous, and silky, about 10 seconds.

Pour batter into prepared pan. Bake cheesecake until deeply golden brown on top and still very jiggly in the center, 60–65 minutes.

Let cool slightly (it will fall drastically as it cools), then unmold. Let cool completely. Carefully peel away parchment from sides of cheesecake. Slice into wedges and serve at room temperature, preferably with a glass of sherry alongside.

Do Ahead: Cheesecake be made 1 day ahead. Cover and chill. Be sure to let cheesecake sit for several hours at room temperature to remove chill before serving.

Ginger-Raspberry Cake

Ingredients

RASPBERRY SAUCE
4 cups fresh raspberries
5 Tbsp. (63 g) sugar
1 Tbsp. finely chopped crystallized ginger
2 Tbsp. cornstarch

CARAMEL CREAM AND ASSEMBLY
1cup (200 g) sugar
3cups heavy cream, divided
35–40 thin ginger cookies (such as Anna's Ginger Swedish Thins)
2¼ cups fresh raspberries, plus more for serving
Assorted fresh currants (for serving; optional)

Preparation
RASPBERRY SAUCE

Cook raspberries, sugar, and ginger in a medium saucepan over medium heat, crushing with a potato masher, until softened and some of the liquid evaporates, 6–8 minutes.

Transfer 3 Tbsp. cooking liquid to a small bowl and whisk in cornstarch. Stir slurry into sauce in pan and cook, stirring, until thickened to about the consistency of jam, about 2 minutes; let cool.

CARAMEL CREAM AND ASSEMBLY

Cook sugar and 3 Tbsp. water in a small saucepan over medium heat, without stirring, until mixture starts to darken in spots. Carefully swirl pan to evenly cook sugar but do not stir it. Cook, swirling occasionally, until caramel is a deep amber, about 8 minutes. Immediately stir in 1 cup cream. Cook until no streaks remain, about 30 seconds. Let cool.

Using an electric mixer on medium-high speed, beat remaining 2 cups cream in a large bowl to medium peaks. Add cooled caramel and beat to stiff peaks (a few swirls of caramel are okay).
Line an 8x8" baking dish with 2 sheets of parchment paper, leaving a 2" overhang on all 4 sides. Cover bottom with a single layer of cookies, breaking to fit as needed. Top with about ½ cup raspberry sauce and spread evenly to corners and edges. Top with ¾ cup raspberries, then spread 2 cups caramel cream over berries. Repeat layers with remaining ingredients. Cover and chill at least 6 hours.

To serve, top with more raspberries and currants (if desired) and slice, wiping knife between cuts.

Do ahead: Icebox cake can be made 2 days ahead. Keep chilled.

Chocolate-Matcha Butter Cake

6 Tbsp. unsalted butter, melted, slightly cooled,
plus room-temperature butter for pan
1½ cups (227 g) mochiko (sweet rice flour; such as
Koda Farms or Bob's Red Mill Sweet White Rice
Flour)
1 tsp. baking powder
½ tsp. Diamond Crystal or ¼ tsp. Morton kosher
salt Tbsp. matcha, sifted, plus more for serving
2 large eggs
1 14-oz. can sweetened condensed milk
1 tsp. vanilla extract
1⅓ cups heavy cream, divided
4 oz. bittersweet chocolate, chopped

Preparation

Place a rack in middle of oven; preheat to 350°. Generously butter an 8"- or 9"-diameter cake pan. Whisk mochiko, baking powder, salt, and 2 Tbsp. matcha in a large bowl just to combine. Vigorously whisk eggs and melted butter in a medium bowl until pale and emulsified, about 30 seconds. Add sweetened condensed milk, vanilla, and 1 cup cream and whisk until mixture is smooth. Scrape into dry ingredients and whisk vigorously until smooth and very thick. Scrape batter into prepared pan and smooth surface.

Bake cake until it starts to pull away from sides of pan, top and edges are golden, and a tester inserted into the center comes out clean, 35–45 minutes (cake in the smaller pan will take longer to bake than one in the larger pan). Transfer pan to a wire rack and let cake cool 5 minutes. Turn cake out onto rack; let cool completely.

Place chocolate in a small heatproof bowl. Bring remaining ⅓ cup cream to a boil in a small saucepan. Immediately pour over chocolate; let sit 15 seconds. Stir until ganache is smooth.

Evenly pour ganache over top of cake. Using a small offset spatula or spoon, spread ganache to edges of cake (drips down the sides are encouraged!). Let sit until ganache is set, about 2 hours. (If you are in a hurry, you can chill cake until glaze is set, about 30 minutes.)

Just before serving, dust top of cake with more Matcha with a fine-mesh sieve.

Do ahead: Cake and glaze can be made 2 days ahead. Store cake tightly wrapped in several layers of plastic at room temperature. Let glaze cool, then chill in an airtight container. Gently reheat glaze in the microwave or a double boiler over a pan of simmering water (do not let bowl touch water) until just melted before using.

Carrot Cake

Ingredients:

For the cake:

2 cups all-purpose flour
2 tsp baking powder
1 1/2 tsp baking soda
1 tsp ground cinnamon
1/2 tsp ground ginger
1/4 tsp ground nutmeg
1/2 tsp salt
1 1/2 cups granulated sugar
1 cup vegetable oil
4 large eggs
2 cups grated carrots
1/2 cup chopped walnuts (optional)

For the cream cheese frosting:

8 oz cream cheese, softened
1/2 cup unsalted butter, softened 2 cups
powdered sugar
1 tsp vanilla extract

Instructions:

Preheat your oven to 350°F (180°C). Grease two 9-inch round cake pans with cooking spray.
In a mixing bowl, whisk together the all-purpose flour, baking powder, baking soda, ground cinnamon, ground ginger, ground nutmeg, and salt.
In a separate bowl, beat together the granulated sugar and vegetable oil until well combined.
Beat in the eggs, one at a time, until well combined.
Gradually stir the dry ingredients into the wet ingredients until well combined and the batter is smooth.
Fold in the grated carrots and chopped walnuts, if using.
Pour the batter into the prepared cake pans and smooth the surface with a spatula.
Bake for 30-35 minutes or until a toothpick inserted into the center of the cake comes out clean.
Allow the cakes to cool in the pans for 10 minutes before transferring them to a wire rack to cool completely. To make the cream cheese frosting, beat together the softened cream cheese and unsalted butter with an electric mixer until light and fluffy.
Gradually beat in the powdered sugar and vanilla extract until well combined and the frosting is smooth and creamy.
Once the cakes are completely cooled, place one cake layer on a cake plate or stand and spread a layer of frosting over the top.
Place the second cake layer on top and spread frosting over the top and sides of the cake.
Decorate the cake with additional chopped walnuts, if desired.
Enjoy your delicious carrot cake!

Yogurt Pound Cake

Ingredients:

2 1/2 cups all-purpose flour 2
tsp baking powder
1/2 tsp baking soda
1/2 tsp salt
1 cup plain Greek yogurt
1 1/2 cups granulated sugar 3
large eggs
1/2 cup vegetable oil
2 tsp vanilla extract
Zest of 1 lemon (optional)

Instructions:

Preheat your oven to 350°F (175°C). Grease a 9x5 inch loaf pan with cooking spray.
In a mixing bowl, whisk together the all-purpose flour, baking powder, baking soda, and salt.
In a separate bowl, mix together the Greek yogurt and granulated sugar until well combined.
Beat in the eggs, one at a time, until well combined.
Mix in the vegetable oil, vanilla extract, and lemon zest (if using) until well combined.
Gradually stir the dry ingredients into the wet ingredients until well combined and the batter is smooth.
Pour the batter into the prepared loaf pan and smooth the surface with a spatula.
Bake for 50-60 minutes or until a toothpick inserted into the center of the cake comes out clean. Allow the yogurt pound cake to cool in the pan for 10 minutes before transferring it to a wire rack to cool completely.
Slice and serve your delicious yogurt pound cake. It's great on its own or with a dusting of powdered sugar or a dollop of whipped cream.
Enjoy your moist and tangy yogurt pound cake!

German Apple Cake

Ingredients:

For the Cake:

2 cups all-purpose flour
1 tsp baking powder
1/2 tsp baking soda
1/2 tsp salt
1/2 cup unsalted butter, softened
1 cup granulated sugar
2 large eggs
1 tsp vanilla extract
1/2 cup milk
2 cups peeled and thinly sliced apples

For the Topping:

1/2 cup granulated sugar
1/2 cup all-purpose flour
1/2 tsp ground cinnamon
1/4 cup unsalted butter, melted

Instructions:

Preheat the oven to 350°F. Grease a 9-inch springform pan with cooking spray.
In a medium bowl, whisk together the flour, baking powder, baking soda, and salt.
In a large mixing bowl, cream the softened butter and sugar until light and fluffy.
Beat in the eggs, one at a time, and add the vanilla extract.
Add the dry ingredients to the butter mixture, alternating with the milk, and mix until well combined.
Fold in the sliced apples.
Pour the batter into the prepared springform pan.
In a small bowl, mix together the sugar, flour, and cinnamon for the topping.
Pour the melted butter over the dry ingredients and mix with a fork until crumbly.
Sprinkle the topping evenly over the cake batter.
Bake the cake for 50-60 minutes or until a toothpick inserted into the center comes out clean.
Allow the cake to cool in the pan for 10-15 minutes.
Run a knife around the edges of the cake to loosen it from the pan.
Remove the sides of the springform pan and transfer the cake to a serving plate.
Slice and serve the German Apple Cake warm or at room temperature.
Enjoy your delicious and fluffy German Apple Cake with a dollop of whipped cream or a scoop of vanilla ice cream!

Margarita Cake

Ingredients:

2 cups all-purpose flour
1 tablespoon baking powder
1/2 teaspoon salt
1/2 cup unsalted butter, softened
1 1/2 cups granulated sugar
4 large eggs
1/2 cup vegetable oil
1/2 cup freshly squeezed lime juice 2
tablespoons tequila
2 tablespoons triple sec

For the glaze:

1/2 cup powdered sugar
1 tablespoon freshly squeezed lime
juice 1 tablespoon tequila
Lime zest, for garnish

Instructions:

Preheat your oven to 350°F. Grease and flour a 9-inch cake pan.
In a medium bowl, whisk together the flour, baking powder, and salt.
In a large bowl, cream together the butter and sugar until light and fluffy. Add the eggs, one at a time, mixing well after each addition.
Gradually add the flour mixture to the butter mixture, alternating with the vegetable oil. Mix until well combined.
Stir in the lime juice, tequila, and triple sec until the batter is smooth.
Pour the batter into the prepared pan and bake for 30-35 minutes, or until a toothpick inserted into the center of the cake comes out clean.
While the cake is baking, make the glaze. In a small bowl, whisk together the powdered sugar, lime juice, and tequila until smooth.
Once the cake is done baking, remove it from the oven and let it cool in the pan for 10 minutes. Then, remove the cake from the pan and transfer it to a wire rack to cool completely.
Drizzle the glaze over the cooled cake and sprinkle with lime zest for garnish.
Enjoy your delicious Margarita Cake!

Coconut Chiffon Cake

Ingredients:

1 1/2 cups cake flour
1 cup sugar
2 tsp baking powder 1/2 tsp salt
1/2 cup vegetable oil 5 large egg yolks
3/4 cup coconut milk 1 tsp vanilla
extract
5 large egg whites
1/2 tsp cream of tartar

For the frosting:

1/2 cup unsalted butter, softened
1/2 cup cream cheese, softened
2 cups powdered sugar
1 tsp vanilla extract
1/4 tsp salt
1/4 cup sweetened shredded coconut,
toasted

Instructions:

Preheat the oven to 325°F (160°C). Grease and flour a 9-inch (23-cm) tube pan.
In a large mixing bowl, sift together the cake flour, sugar, baking powder, and salt.
Add the vegetable oil, egg yolks, coconut milk, and vanilla extract to the dry ingredients. Beat
with an electric mixer on medium speed until smooth and well blended.
In another large mixing bowl, beat the egg whites and cream of tartar until stiff peaks form.
Gently fold the egg whites into the batter in three additions.
Pour the batter into the prepared pan and smooth the top with a spatula.
Bake for 45-50 minutes or until a toothpick inserted into the center of the cake comes out
clean. Remove from the oven and invert the pan onto a wire rack. Let the cake cool
completely in the pan.
To make the frosting, beat the butter and cream cheese together until smooth.
Gradually add the powdered sugar, vanilla extract, and salt, beating until the mixture is light
and fluffy.
Frost the top and sides of the cake with the frosting.
Sprinkle the toasted coconut on top of the frosting.
Serve and enjoy your delicious Coconut Chiffon Cake!

Dutch Apple Cake

Ingredients:

1 1/2 cups all-purpose flour
1 teaspoon baking powder
1/2 teaspoon salt
1/2 teaspoon cinnamon
1/4 teaspoon nutmeg
1/2 cup unsalted butter, room
temperature 1 cup granulated sugar
2 large eggs
1 teaspoon vanilla extract
3 medium apples, peeled, cored and
sliced 2 tablespoons lemon juice
1/4 cup brown sugar
1/4 cup all-purpose flour
1/2 teaspoon cinnamon
1/4 cup unsalted butter, cold and cubed

Instructions:

Preheat your oven to 350°F (175°C). Grease and flour a 9-inch cake pan.
In a medium bowl, whisk together the flour, baking powder, salt, cinnamon, and nutmeg.
In a separate large mixing bowl, beat the butter and granulated sugar until creamy and fluffy.
Add in the eggs one at a time, mixing well after each addition. Stir in the vanilla extract.
Gradually add the flour mixture to the wet ingredients, mixing until just combined.
In a separate bowl, mix the sliced apples and lemon juice together.
Pour the cake batter into the prepared cake pan. Arrange the sliced apples over the top of the cake.
In a small bowl, mix together the brown sugar, flour, cinnamon, and cold cubed butter. Using your hands, mix the ingredients together until crumbly.
Sprinkle the crumb topping over the apples.
Bake the cake in the preheated oven for 45-50 minutes, or until a toothpick inserted into the center of the cake comes out clean.
Allow the cake to cool for 10-15 minutes in the pan, then transfer it to a wire rack to cool completely.
Serve the Dutch Apple Cake warm or at room temperature, garnished with a dollop of whipped cream or a dusting of powdered sugar, if desired. Enjoy!

Moist Chocolate Cake

Ingredients:

1 3/4 cups all-purpose flour
2 cups granulated sugar
3/4 cup unsweetened cocoa
powder 2 teaspoons baking soda
1 teaspoon baking powder
1 teaspoon salt
1 cup buttermilk
1/2 cup vegetable oil
2 large eggs
2 teaspoons vanilla extract
1 cup hot water

Instructions:

Preheat your oven to 350°F (175°C) and grease a 9-inch round cake pan.
In a large mixing bowl, combine the flour, sugar, cocoa powder, baking soda, baking powder, and salt.
In a separate bowl, whisk together the buttermilk, vegetable oil, eggs, and vanilla extract until well combined.
Add the wet ingredients to the dry ingredients and mix until just combined.
Add the hot water to the batter and mix until well combined. The batter will be thin, but that's okay.
Pour the batter into the prepared cake pan.
Bake for 30-35 minutes or until a toothpick inserted into the center of the cake comes out clean.
Let the cake cool in the pan for 10 minutes before removing it from the pan and placing it on a wire rack to cool completely.
Serve the cake as is or frost it with your favorite frosting.
Enjoy your deliciously moist chocolate cake!

Lemon Sour Cream Pound Cake

Ingredients:

1 1/2 cups all-purpose flour
1/2 tsp baking powder
1/4 tsp baking soda
1/4 tsp salt
1/2 cup unsalted butter, softened
1 cup granulated sugar
2 large eggs
1/2 cup sour cream
1 tbsp finely grated lemon zest
1 tbsp freshly squeezed lemon
juice 1 tsp vanilla extract

Instructions:

Preheat the oven to 350°F (180°C). Grease and flour an 8-inch loaf pan.
In a medium bowl, whisk together the flour, baking powder, baking soda, and salt.
In a large bowl, beat the butter and sugar together until light and fluffy, about 3-4 minutes.
Add the eggs one at a time, beating well after each addition.
Add the sour cream, lemon zest, lemon juice, and vanilla extract and mix well.
Add the dry ingredients to the wet ingredients and mix until just combined.
Pour the batter into the prepared loaf pan and smooth the top with a spatula.
Bake for 50-60 minutes or until a toothpick inserted into the center comes out clean. Let the cake cool in the pan for 10 minutes, then remove it from the pan and transfer it to a wire rack to cool completely.
Serve and enjoy!
Optional: You can make a simple glaze by mixing 1 cup of powdered sugar and 2-3 tablespoons of lemon juice. Drizzle the glaze over the cooled cake for added sweetness and tanginess.

Brown Sugar & Chocolate Swirl Cheesecake

Ingredients:

2 cups graham cracker crumbs
1/2 cup unsalted butter, melted
1/4 cup granulated sugar
4 (8 oz) packages cream cheese, softened
1 1/4 cups light brown sugar, packed 4
large eggs
2 tsp vanilla extract
1/2 cup semi-sweet chocolate chips,
melted

Instructions:

Preheat oven to 325°F (163°C).
In a bowl, combine the graham cracker crumbs, melted butter, and granulated sugar. Mix until well combined.
Press the mixture into the bottom and up the sides of a 9-inch springform pan.
In a large mixing bowl, beat the cream cheese and brown sugar together until creamy and smooth.
Add the eggs, one at a time, mixing well after each addition.
Stir in the vanilla extract.
Remove 1 cup of the cheesecake batter and stir in the melted chocolate chips until well combined.
Pour half of the remaining plain cheesecake batter over the crust in the prepared pan.
Spoon half of the chocolate cheesecake batter over the plain cheesecake batter. Use a knife to gently swirl the two batters together.
Repeat with the remaining plain and chocolate cheesecake batters.
Place the cheesecake pan onto a large baking sheet and bake for 50-60 minutes or until the center of the cheesecake is almost set.
Remove the cheesecake from the oven and let it cool to room temperature.
Chill the cheesecake in the refrigerator for at least 4 hours or overnight.
Serve the cheesecake chilled and enjoy!
Note: If desired, you can decorate the top of the cheesecake with additional melted chocolate or whipped cream before serving.

Butter Pecan Cake

Ingredients:

2 cups of all-purpose flour
1 teaspoon of baking powder
1/2 teaspoon of baking soda
1/2 teaspoon of salt
1 cup of unsalted butter,
softened 2 cups of granulated
sugar
4 large eggs
1 cup of buttermilk
1 tablespoon of vanilla extract
1/2 cup of chopped pecans
For the frosting:

1/2 cup of unsalted butter,
softened 8 ounces of cream
cheese, softened 1 teaspoon of
vanilla extract
3 cups of powdered sugar
1/2 cup of chopped pecans

Instructions:

Preheat the oven to 350°F (175°C). Grease and flour two 9-inch cake pans.
In a medium bowl, whisk together the flour, baking powder, baking soda, and salt.
In a large mixing bowl, cream the butter and sugar until light and fluffy.
Add the eggs, one at a time, beating well after each addition.
Mix in the buttermilk and vanilla extract.
Add the flour mixture to the wet ingredients, a little at a time, and mix until just combined.
Fold in the chopped pecans.
Pour the batter into the prepared cake pans and bake for 25-30 minutes, or until a toothpick inserted
into the center of the cakes comes out clean.
Let the cakes cool completely in the pans before removing and frosting.
To make the frosting, cream together the butter and cream cheese until smooth
Add the vanilla extract and mix until combined.
Gradually add the powdered sugar, mixing until the frosting is light and fluffy.
Fold in the chopped pecans.
Frost the cooled cake with the butter pecan frosting and serve. Enjoy!

Hazelnut Cake Squares

Ingredients:

1 cup all-purpose flour
1/2 cup hazelnuts, toasted and
finely chopped
1/2 cup unsalted butter, at room
temperature
1/2 cup granulated sugar
1 egg
1/2 teaspoon vanilla extract
1/4 teaspoon salt
1/4 teaspoon baking powder
For the glaze:

1/2 cup powdered sugar
2 tablespoons milk
1/4 teaspoon vanilla
extract

Instructions:

Preheat the oven to 350°F. Grease an 8-inch square baking pan.
In a medium bowl, whisk together the flour, hazelnuts, salt, and baking powder.
In a separate bowl, using an electric mixer, beat the butter and granulated sugar
together until light and fluffy. Add the egg and vanilla extract and beat until smooth.
Add the dry ingredients to the butter mixture and beat until just combined.
Spread the batter evenly into the prepared baking pan.
Bake for 20-25 minutes or until a toothpick inserted into the center comes out clean.
While the cake is baking, make the glaze. In a small bowl, whisk together the powdered
sugar, milk, and vanilla extract until smooth.
Let the cake cool in the pan for 10 minutes, then remove it from the pan and let it cool
completely on a wire rack.
Once the cake has cooled, drizzle the glaze over the top. Cut the cake into squares and
serve. Enjoy!

Blueberry Ricotta Pound Cake

Ingredients

1 ⅔ Cups (205 g) All-Purpose Flour.
1 Tablespoon Baking Powder.
1 teaspoon Sea Salt.
1 ⅔ Cups (370 g) Whole Milk Ricotta.
¾ Cup (170 g) Unsalted Butter, softened. 1 ½ Cups (300 g) Granulated Sugar.
1 Lemon's worth of zest.
3 (150 g) Eggs, large.

This Blueberry Ricotta Pound Cake is a delicious and healthy dessert for kids. It's packed with creamy ricotta cheese and bursting with fresh blueberries. The cake is made using all-purpose flour, baking powder, sea salt, whole milk ricotta, unsalted butter, granulated sugar, lemon zest, and eggs. The combination of these ingredients creates a moist and fluffy pound cake that your kids will love! For added flavor and texture, top the cake off with some extra fresh or frozen blueberries. Serve it as an after-dinner treat or enjoy it for breakfast! No matter when you have it, this Blueberry Ricotta Pound Cake is sure to be enjoyed by all. Enjoy!

Happy baking!

Yogurt Cake

This no-sugar dessert recipe is sure to please! An easy and healthy way to get your sweet treat fix without breaking the calorie bank, this yogurt cake is made with just four simple ingredients. Start by preheating your oven to 350 degrees Fahrenheit. In a large bowl, combine the cake mix, Greek yogurt, and water until everything is completely combined and no lumps remain. Grease a 9x13 inch pan and pour in the batter evenly. Bake for 25- 30 minutes or until a toothpick inserted into the center of the cake comes out clean. Let cool before frosting with Cool Whip, if desired. Enjoy your delicious no sugar dessert! With this recipe, you can have your cake and eat it too!

This no sugar dessert recipe is a great way to indulge without the guilt. Perfect for parties or just an everyday indulgence, this yogurt cake is sure to be a crowd pleaser. It's so easy to make and no one will ever know that it's sugar-free! Try this no sugar dessert recipe today and enjoy a healthy, delicious treat. Your taste buds will thank you!

Blueberry Coffee Cake

INGREDIENTS

¾ CUP BUTTER, MELTED AND COOLED, GREAT
VALUE SWEET CREAM SALTED BUTTER, 16 OZ.
1 CUP MILK,
3 EGGS,
1 TEASPOON VANILLA EXTRACT,
1 ½ CUPS GRANULAR SUCROLOSE SWEETENER
(SUCH AS SPLENDA®)
2 TEASPOONS BAKING POWDER,
3 CUPS ALL-PURPOSE FLOUR,
1 ¾ CUPS FRESH OR FROZEN BLUEBERRIES.

This no-sugar recipe for blueberry coffee cake is a delicious and healthy dessert that's easy to prepare. To begin, preheat the oven to 350 degrees F (175 degrees C). In a medium bowl, cream together the melted butter, milk, eggs, and vanilla extract until smooth. In a separate bowl, mix together the sucrolose sweetener, baking powder, and flour. Add the wet ingredients to the dry and mix until evenly combined. Gently fold in the fresh or frozen blueberries.

Grease a nine-inch round cake pan with butter or margarine, then pour the batter into it. Bake for 30 minutes, or until a tester inserted into the center of the cake comes out clean. Let cool before serving. Enjoy your no-sugar blueberry coffee cake as a healthy dessert!

This no-sugar blueberry coffee cake is sure to be a hit with everyone and make great leftovers for breakfast or snacks through the week. After baking, let cool before serving. Enjoy your no-sugar blueberry coffee cake as a healthy dessert that's sure to be a hit with everyone!

Chocolate Brownie Cake

Ingredients
100g butter
125g caster sugar
75g light brown or muscovado sugar
125g plain chocolate (plain or milk)
1 tbsp golden syrup
2 eggs
1 tsp vanilla extract/essence
100g plain flour
½ tsp baking powder
2 tbsp cocoa powder

If you're looking for a simple yet delicious kid-friendly dessert recipe, a chocolate brownie cake is the perfect choice. Not only does it look and taste amazing, but it's easy to make too! All you need are some basic ingredients such as butter, caster sugar, light brown or muscovado sugar, plain chocolate of your choice (plain or milk), golden syrup, eggs, vanilla extract/essence, plain flour, baking powder and cocoa powder. Simply mix all the ingredients together in a bowl until well combined. You can even get your little ones involved to help make this delightful treat for the whole family! Once baked, you'll have yourself a delicious chocolate brownie cake that everyone will enjoy! Kid-friendly desserts have never been so easy and delicious. Try out this chocolate brownie cake recipe today for a fun, sweet treat!

Ricotta Cake

INGREDIENTS
200g unsalted butter, chilled, chopped
1 3/4 cup (385g) caster sugar
5 eggs
3 cups (450g) plain flour
1 tsp baking powder
700g fresh ricotta
500g cream cheese, at room temperature
2 tsp vanilla extract
Pure icing sugar, to dust

Ricotta cake is a delicious dessert that can be easily prepared at home. It's one of those dessert ideas you can make without much fuss and it tastes great! The dessert starts with the basic ingredients: unsalted butter, caster sugar, eggs, plain flour, baking powder, fresh ricotta, cream cheese and vanilla extract.
All these ingredients are combined to make a soft, light and creamy cake.

To prepare the dessert, first preheat the oven to 180C/160C fan-forced. Grease a 20cm round springform tin and line with baking paper. Beat butter and sugar in a bowl until light and creamy then add eggs one at a time, beating after each addition. Add sifted flour and baking powder and stir until just combined.

Spread half of the mixture into the prepared tin. In a separate bowl mix together ricotta, cream cheese and vanilla extract then spread over base in the tin. Top with remaining cake mixture and smooth top evenly. Bake for 1 hour or until a skewer inserted into the cake comes out clean.

Let the dessert sit in tin for 10 minutes before transferring to a wire rack to cool completely. When you're ready to serve, dust the top of the ricotta cake with pure icing sugar. Enjoy your dessert!

Rhubarb Custard Cake

Ingredients
8 servings
4 Tbsp. melted unsalted butter, cooled, plus
more room-temperature for pan
1 cup all-purpose flour, plus more for pan
¾ tsp. baking powder
½ tsp. kosher salt
2 large eggs
1 large egg yolk
1½ cups sugar, plus more for sprinkling
¼ cup sour cream
2 Tbsp. dark rum
2 tsp. finely grated lemon zest
13 oz. rhubarb stalks, halved lengthwise if
thick

Preparation

Preheat oven to 350°. Butter and flour pan. Whisk baking powder, salt, and 1 cup all-purpose flour in a medium bowl. Whisk eggs, egg yolk, and 1½ cups sugar in a large bowl until very pale and thick, about 1 minute. Whisk melted butter, sour cream, rum, and lemon zest in a small bowl. Whisk butter mixture into egg mixture just to combine. Add dry ingredients and fold in until batter is smooth; scrape into prepared pan. Chill 10 minutes to let batter set.

Arrange rhubarb over batter however you like, trimming as needed. Don't press fruit into batter—just place over top and let it rest on the surface. Sprinkle with more sugar and bake until cake is golden on top and browned around the sides, 45–55 minutes. Transfer pan to a wire rack and let cake cool in pan 10 minutes. Slide a knife around sides of cake to loosen and unmold. Slide directly onto rack and let cool completely.

Do Ahead: Cake can be baked 1 day ahead. Store tightly wrapped at room temperature.

Black Sesame Mochi Cake With Caramel

Ingredients

Makes one 8" or 9" cake

¼ cup (½ stick) unsalted butter, melted, plus
more for pan
¾ cup (3.6 oz.) black sesame seeds
1¼ cups sugar, divided
2 cups (254 g) glutinous sweet rice flour
(preferably Koda Farms Mochiko)
1 tsp. baking powder
1 tsp. kosher salt, divided
2 large eggs
1 cup whole milk
1 tsp. vanilla extract
½ cup plus 5 Tbsp. heavy cream
Pinch of cream of tartar
Toasted white sesame seeds (for sprinkling)

Preparation

Place a rack in center of oven; preheat to 350°. Generously grease an 8" or 9" round pan with butter. Line bottom with parchment and grease parchment with butter.

Toast black sesame seeds in a dry large skillet over medium heat, stirring frequently, until fragrant and just starting to crackle, 2–3 minutes. Transfer to a food processor or blender. Pulse, scraping down sides as needed, until seeds are finely chopped but haven't formed a paste. This could take as long as 2–3 minutes in a food processor, or 1–2 minutes in a high-speed blender.

Scoop out ¼ cup ground sesame seeds; set aside. Add ¾ cup sugar to food processor and pulse until sugar is a uniform gray and no lumps of sesame remain. Transfer to a large bowl. Sprinkle some sesame sugar all over sides and bottom of prepared pan (as if you were flouring it). Tap pan so sesame sugar coats sides and bottom in a thin layer; this will form a crust, which will help the cake release. Tap out any excess back into bowl. Add flour, baking powder, and ½ tsp. salt to bowl and whisk to combine.

Whisk eggs and ¼ cup melted butter in a medium bowl until creamy and emulsified, about 30 seconds. Whisk in milk, vanilla, and ½ cup cream. Add egg mixture to dry ingredients and stir to combine.

Transfer batter to prepared pan. Bake cake until a tester inserted into the center comes out clean and cake is risen and springy with a firm golden brown crust, 45–55 minutes (the smaller your pan, the longer it will take). Run a knife or offset spatula around edge of pan. Let cake cool in pan 10 minutes before inverting onto a wire rack. Invert again onto another wire rack and let cool completely.

Vigorously whisk reserved ¼ cup ground sesame seeds with remaining 5 Tbsp. cream and ½ tsp. salt in a medium bowl until smooth.

Bring cream of tartar, remaining ½ cup sugar, and 3 Tbsp. water to a boil in large skillet over medium-high heat, stirring to dissolve sugar. Cook, stirring frequently, until mixture is the color of light honey, 3–4 minutes. Immediately remove caramel from heat. Vigorously whisk in cream mixture until combined. Immediately pour onto center of cooled cake and spread to the edges. Garnish circumference of cake with white sesame seeds.

Blueberry-Lemon Icebox Cake

Ingredients

8 ounces mascarpone or plain
whole-milk Greek yogurt, room
temperature
¾ cup powdered sugar
2 tablespoons finely grated lemon
zest
2½ cups chilled heavy cream
1 cup homemade or store-bought
lemon curd, divided
16 graham crackers, divided
1½ cups Blueberry-Chia Seed Jam,
divided
⅓ cup fresh blueberries

Preparation

Line a 9x5" loaf pan with plastic wrap, leaving overhang on all sides. Using an electric mixer on medium-high speed, beat mascarpone, powdered sugar, and lemon zest in a large bowl until fluffy, about 4 minutes. Reduce speed to low; gradually add cream. Increase speed to medium as mixture thickens; beat until medium peaks form. Transfer two-thirds of mascarpone mixture to another large bowl and fold in ½ cup lemon curd. Cover remaining mascarpone mixture; chill until ready to unmold and cover cake.

Place a single layer of graham crackers over bottom of prepared pan, breaking as needed to fit. Using a small offset spatula, evenly spread a quarter of lemon cream over graham crackers. Dollop ½ cup jam over top, then gently spread evenly over lemon cream. Drizzle ¼ cup lemon curd over. Spoon a third of remaining lemon cream over curd and top with another layer of graham crackers. Repeat layering process with half of remaining lemon cream, ½ cup jam, and remaining lemon curd. Finish with a final layer of lemon cream, then graham crackers. Cover with plastic wrap; freeze at least 6 hours. Cover and chill remaining jam until ready to serve cake.

Uncover cake and invert pan onto a platter. Using the plastic overhang to help you, unmold cake; peel off plastic. Spread top and sides of cake with reserved mascarpone mixture (if mixture looks a little loose, whisk until soft peaks form before using). Chill in freezer at least 15 minutes. Just before serving, mix blueberries into reserved jam and spoon over cake.

Do Ahead: Cake can be made 2 days ahead. Cover and keep frozen.

Plum and Almond Cake

Ingredients

Nonstick vegetable oil spray
1 cup all-purpose flour
½ cup almond meal
1½ teaspoons baking powder
½ teaspoon kosher salt
½ cup (1 stick) unsalted butter, room
temperature
¾ cup granulated sugar
¼ cup brown sugar
2 large eggs
1 teaspoon finely grated orange zest
1 teaspoon vanilla paste or vanilla
extract
14 Italian plums, halved, seeded
2 tablespoons demarara sugar
Powdered sugar (for dusting)

Preparation

Preheat oven to 350°. Generously coat a 10" cake or springform pan with nonstick spray. Whisk flour, almond meal, baking powder, and salt in a medium bowl. Using an electric mixer on medium speed, beat butter, granulated sugar, and brown sugar in a large bowl until pale and creamy, about 4 minutes. Add eggs one at a time, mixing well to incorporate after each addition, then add orange zest and vanilla paste and beat until fully incorporated, about 3 minutes. Reduce speed to low and gradually add dry ingredients; beat just until smooth and no lumps remain, about 30 seconds.

Scrape batter into prepared pan and arrange plums, cut side down, on top of batter, taking care not to push the plums into the batter (the batter will rise as it bakes, slightly submerging them). Sprinkle demarara sugar over and bake cake until top is golden brown, plums are very soft, and a tester inserted into the center comes out clean, 50–60 minutes. Transfer to a wire rack and let cake cool in pan at least 30 minutes. Run a sharp knife around sides of pan to loosen cake. Carefully invert cake onto a rimmed baking sheet, then invert again onto a platter or cake stand. Dust with powdered sugar just before serving.

Do Ahead: Cake can be made 8 hours ahead. Cover tightly and let stand at room temperature.

Pineapple Upside Down Cake

Ingredients

TOPPING:

565g/ 20 oz canned pineapple slices in juice (not in syrup, Note 1)
12 - 18+ maraschino cherries (Note 2)
60g/ 4 tbsp unsalted butter , melted
1/2 cup brown sugar

CAKE:

1 1/2 cups flour
1 tsp baking powder
1/4 tsp baking soda (sub 1 tsp baking powder)
1/4 tsp salt
1/3 cup milk , full or low-fat
1/4 cup pineapple juice , reserved from can (under Topping ingredients)
1/4 cup sour cream , full fat (sub plain yogurt)
1 tsp vanilla extract (or essence)
115g/ 1 stick butter , unsalted, softened (to 18C/64F. Note 3)
3/4 cup white sugar
2 large eggs , at room temperature (Note 4)
Any leftover pineapple , chopped (Note 1)

Instructions

Preheat oven to 180°C/350°F (160°C fan).

PINEAPPLE DECORATIVE TOP:

Dry fruits: Line a tray with paper towels or a tea towel, then place pineapple and cherries on. Pat dry with paper towels.

Butter: Pour melted butter into a 23cm/9" cake pan at least 5cm/2" deep. (Not springform, as they'll leak) Brush butter up the sides.

Brown sugar: Sprinkle sugar over the base, roughly spreading it out (use the brush).

Arrange pineapple: Place one pineapple ring in the centre, then surround with either halved pineapple rings (as pictured), or whole ones.

Decorate with cherries as desired. Most people just put them in the middle of the pineapple rings.

Press cherries and pineapples down firmly so they are in direct contact with the base of the cake pan – so you get vibrant red and yellow colour pops at the end, not tarnished by caramel. (Note 5)

BATTER:

Flour Mixture: Whisk flour, baking powder, baking soda and salt in a bowl.

Milk Mixture: Whisk milk, sour cream, pineapple juice and vanilla in a 2nd bowl.

Cream butter and sugar: In a third (final!) bowl, beat the butter and sugar for 2 minutes on speed 7 (handheld mixer) until fluffy.

Eggs: Add eggs one at a time, beating for 20 seconds in between.

Add Flour Mixture then Milk Mixture, alternating: Add 1/3 of the Flour Mixture, then mix in using a rubber spatula. Add 1/2 the Milk Mixture, mix in. Add half the remaining Flour Mixture, mix. Add all the remaining Milk Mixture, mix. Then mix in the last of the Flour Mixture. Stir in the leftover pineapple pieces.

Fill pan: Spread batter over pineapple layer, smooth and level the surface.

Bake: Bake for 30 minutes. Remove, loosely cover with foil, then bake for a further 15 minutes until a toothpick inserted into the centre comes out clean.

TURNING OUT CAKE:

Cool 20 minutes: Remove cake from oven and leave inside pan to cool for 20 minutes.

Flip! Run a butter knife around the inner edge of the cake pan. Put a plate or serving platter over the cake, then flip. Tap base / shake pan gently then lift slowly. Voila!

Cool completely before serving.

Recipe Notes:

1. Pineapple slices – Be sure to get pineapple in juice, not syrup. Syrup is too sweet and also the cake batter calls for pineapple juice.

Cans: In Australia, the standard can sizes are 430g and 225g, so get one of each. Total 655g, which is more than needed. Chop up the leftover pineapple and add into the batter.

2. Maraschino cherries – Preserved, sweetened cherries commonly associated as a cocktail garnish! Find them at liquor stores or Harris Farms (Sydney/QLD). Glacé cherries also work!

3. Softened butter – Don't let the butter get too soft and sloppy. This is a common error with cakes that call for butter and sugar to be creamed. Target 18C/64F for the butter. At this temperature, the butter is loose enough to be whipped, but you should not be left with a thick, shiny slick of grease on your finger when you poke it. If you get greasy fingers, this means the butter is too soft. The cake will not be as fluffy as intended, or the batter might split and be greasy.

If the butter is >20C/68F, I would chill the butter a bit before using.

4. Eggs – Eggs need to be at room temperature and not fridge-cold, to ensure it incorporates properly into the batter. A quick way to warm up fridge-cold eggs: Place eggs in a large bowl, cover with warm tap water (just warm, not hot) and leave for 5 minutes. Wipe dry (to avoid residual water dripping into bowl), then use per recipe.

Large eggs: 50 – 55g / 2 oz per egg is the industry standard of sizes sold as 'large eggs' in Australia and the US. If your eggs are significantly larger or smaller in size, just weigh different eggs and use 200 – 220g / 8 oz in total (including shell) or 180 – 200g / 7.3 oz in total excluding shell (this is useful if you need to use a partial egg to make up the total required weight. Crack eggs, beat whites and yolks together, THEN pour into a bowl to measure out what you need).

5. Pressing the pineapple and cherries down firmly means their presentation side won't be coated as much in brown caramel, letting the colours shine through more visibly.

6. Optional extra glossy shine for presentation purposes: Corn syrup (warmed), or apricot jam (warm, loosen slightly with water). Brush onto the pineapple and cherry surface after turning out cake.

7. Storage – Keeps in the fridge for at least 5 days. Be sure to bring to room temperature before serving. Nobody wants cold cake!

8. Nutrition per slice, assuming 12 slices.

Oreo Cake

Ingredients

2 ½ cups (315 g) all-purpose flour[1]
2 cups (400 g) granulated sugar
1 Tablespoon baking powder
1 teaspoon salt
6 Tablespoons (85 g) unsalted butter softened to room temperature
⅔ cup (157 ml) canola oil or vegetable oil
½ cup (120 g) sour cream
1 Tablespoon clear vanilla[2]
¾ cup (175 ml) whole milk room temperature preferred
6 large or extra large egg whites[3], room temperature preferred (see note for suggestions on recipes to try with leftover egg yolks.)
20 Oreo cookies broken into pieces
Cream Cheese Frosting [4]
¾ cup (170 g) unsalted butter softened, use full-fat brick-style cream cheese
12 oz cream cheese softened
5 ¼ cup (655 g) powdered sugar
¼ teaspoon salt
1 ½ teaspoons clear vanilla extract
1 Tablespoon heavy cream optional
10 Oreo cookies pulverized to fine crumbs (if any significant pieces remain they will clog your piping tip)
Recommended Equipment
8″ cake pans
Mixing bowls
Ateco 848 Piping Tip
Cook Mode
Prevent your screen from going dark

Instructions

Preheat your oven to 350F (175C) and prepare three 8-inch round cake pans (see note 5 to make in two pans) by lining the bottom of each pan with a round of parchment paper and greasing the sides with baking spray.

In the bowl of a stand mixer (or in a large bowl using an electric mixer) whisk together flour, sugar, baking powder, and salt.

2 ½ cups (315 g) all-purpose flour[1]2 cups (400 g) granulated sugar,1 Tablespoon baking powder,1 teaspoon salt

Turn mixer to low-speed and add butter, one tablespoon at a time, not adding the next tablespoon until the first is completely combined. When you're finished, the mixture should resemble coarse sandy crumbs (see video above for visual).

6 Tablespoons (85 g) unsalted butter softened to room temperature

Add canola oil and stir until combined, then add sour cream and vanilla extract and stir on low-speed until completely combined. With mixer still on low-speed, add milk until combined.

⅔ cup (157 ml) canola oil or vegetable oil,½ cup (120 g) sour cream,1 Tablespoon clear vanilla[2],¾ cup (175 ml) whole milk room temperature preferred

In a separate bowl that is completely clean, dry, and grease-free, use clean, dry beaters to beat egg whites to stiff peaks (I show a visual of this in the post above and in the video if it's your first time doing this!).

6 large or extra large egg whites[3].

Use a spatula to gently fold your whipped egg whites into batter (don't overmix, but make sure there are no lumps of egg white remaining).

Carefully fold in broken Oreo pieces. Divide batter evenly into prepared baking pans and transfer to 350F (175C) oven and bake for 30-35 minutes or until the tops spring back if lightly touched and a toothpick inserted in the center comes out clean or with a few moist crumbs. If your oven does not bake evenly you may need to rotate pans halfway through baking.

20 Oreo cookies

Allow cakes to cool in pan for 15 minutes then carefully invert onto cooling rack and allow to completely cool before assembling and decorating.

Cream Cheese Frosting (makes enough to decorate cake as seen in photos)

Prepare frosting by creaming together butter and cream cheese with an electric mixer or stand mixer until creamy and well-combined.

¾ cup (170 g) unsalted butter,12 oz cream cheese

Gradually add powdered sugar with mixer on low-speed (or see my video for a tip for adding all the sugar at once without making a mess!), scrape the sides and bottom of the bowl, and stir in salt and vanilla extract. With mixer on low speed, add cream and gradually increase mixer speed to high. Beat for 15-30 seconds until light and smooth.

5 ¼ cup (655 g) powdered sugar,¼ teaspoon salt,1 ½ teaspoons clear vanilla extract,1 Tablespoon heavy cream

Evenly ice cake (you'll only need approximately ⅔ of the icing for this), and once whole cake is covered in icing use your hands to press pulverized Oreo crumbs evenly halfway up the cake. Pour about 3-4 Tablespoons of remaining Oreo cookie crumbs into remaining frosting and stir to combine (you can adjust how many crumbs you'd like to use according to how light or dark you would like your frosting to be). Fit a large piping bag with Ateco 848 piping tip and fill with frosting. Pipe swirls around the top of the cake. Serve and enjoy.

10 Oreo cookies

Raspberry Tiramisu Cake

Ingredients
Sponge Cake:

6 large eggs
1 cup white granulated sugar
1 tsp vanilla extract
1 cup all-purpose flour
1 tsp baking powder

Vanilla Pastry Cream:
1 1/2 cups whole milk
1 tablespoon all-purpose flour
3 large egg yolks
1/3 cup white granulated sugar
2 tbsp corn starch
2 tbsp water
1/2 cup unsalted butter
1 tsp vanilla extract
8 oz cream cheese or mascarpone, softened
2 cups heavy cream, chilled
1 cup confectioner's sugar
1 tbsp raspberry liqueur
2 1/2 tsp unflavored gelatin, 1 packet
2 tbsp water

For Cake:
½ to ¾ cup raspberry liqueur
½ cup raspberry preserves
4 to 5 cups fresh raspberries
24 ladyfinger cookies

Instructions
For Vanilla Sponge Cake Layers:

The sponge cake layers and the vanilla pastry cream need to cool completely before being used to assemble the cake. They can be prepared the night before. For the sponge cake, line two, 8-inch (20-cm) cake pans with parchment paper: do not grease the sides. Preheat the oven to 350F/177C. If you don't want a super tall cake, prepare this cake recipe as a two-layer, 10-inch cake.

Place the eggs, sugar and vanilla into a mixer bowl and whisk on high speed for 7 to 9 minutes, until the eggs are thick, pale and voluminous. In a separate bowl, combine the dry ingredients: flour and baking powder. Once the eggs are ready, sift the dry ingredients into the eggs in small increments or one-third at a time. Using a spatula, fold the flour gently but thoroughly into the eggs, mixing from the bottom of the mixing bowl.

Divide the cake batter evenly between the prepared pans. Bake in the preheated oven for 20 to 22 minutes, or until the top of the cake turns a rich, golden-brown color. Immediately after removing the cake from the oven, run a knife along the edge of the pan to release the cake. This will allow it stay level as it cools. Allow the cake layers to cool completely on a wire rack.

Making the Vanilla Pastry Cream:

For the vanilla pastry cream: Place the milk into a medium-sized saucepan and whisk the flour in until no clumps remain. Cook the milk over medium-low heat for approximately 5 minutes, until the milk is steaming hot but not boiling. Meanwhile, in a separate bowl, whisk the eggs and sugar together for a few minutes until the mixture is thick and pale. If the mixture is too thick, add 1 teaspoon of water. In a small ramekin, combine the cornstarch and water, then add this slurry to the egg yolk mixture and whisk briefly.

Slowly temper the hot milk into the egg yolk mixture, whisking for about 30 seconds in between additions. Once the two mixtures have been combined together, pour it back into the saucepan. Cook the custard over medium heat, running a rubber spatula along the bottom the entire time to keep the custard from burning. Cook for 4 to 5 minutes, until a thick pudding forms. It should hold its shape on the back of a spoon. If any clumps form, give the custard a quick whisk. Remove the custard from the heat and add the butter and vanilla, then whisk until the butter is completely melted. Cover the custard with a lid or plastic wrap and cool completely in the refrigerator.

Making the Tiramisu Filling:

For the tiramisu filling: once the custard is cooled, prepare the filling. Place the softened cream cheese or mascarpone into a large mixing bowl and whisk for a few minutes until it's smooth and creamy. Next, add in the confectioner's sugar, raspberry liqueur and heavy cream. Whisk for 4 to 5 minutes until stiff peaks form. In a small ramekin, combine the gelatin and water and stir until well combined. Microwave the gelatin for about 30 seconds, until it's dissolved. The mixture will be hot! Do not wait for the gelatin to cool!! Add the hot gelatin into the whipped cream and whisk for about 30 seconds.

Start adding the chilled custard, about 1 cup at a time, and fold gently but thoroughly after each addition, keeping the whipped cream fluffy.

Assembling the Cake:

To assemble the cake, line the sides of a springform pan with an acetate cake collar or foil. Split each sponge cake layer in half using a sharp serrated knife, creating 4 layers total. Drop the first sponge cake layer into the bottom of the pan and soak it lightly with raspberry liqueur. Next, add a few tablespoons of raspberry preserves and spread evenly to the edges. Add about 1 cup (240 ml) of the tiramisu filling, spreading it evenly to the edges. Next, add a layer of fresh raspberries, about 25 to 30 per layer. Add more cream over the raspberries to seal them in. Watch my video recipe to see how I put the cake together!

Top the raspberry layer with the next sponge cake and repeat the process. For the final layer, first soak the cake lightly with liqueur, then invert onto the top. Add the remaining cream on top and garnish with a layer of fresh raspberries.

Refrigerate the cake overnight to allow the filling to set. When ready to enjoy, unlock the springform pan and transfer the cake onto a stand. Watch my video recipe to see how I do it. Remove the plastic wrap and garnish the sides of the cake with ladyfinger cookies. If desired, wrap the cake with a ribbon for additional garnish.

Mango Cake

Ingredients
For the Easy Sponge Cake:
6 large eggs, room temp
1 cup granulated sugar
1 cup all-purpose flour
1/2 tsp baking powder
For the Mango Cake Filling/ Topping:
1 lb fresh mangos, (2 medium) peeled and thinly sliced
into strips
1 lb fresh mangos, (2 medium) 1 1/2 cups puréed
1 to 4 Tbsp sugar, if needed
For the Cream Cheese Frosting:
16 oz cream cheese, 2 packages, softened
1 cup unsalted butter, (16 Tbsp), softened
2 1/2 cups powdered sugar
2 tsp vanilla extract

Instructions
Prep: Pre-heat oven to 350°F. Line the bottoms of two 9" cake pans with parchment (do not grease).
In the bowl of a stand mixer fitted with whisk, beat 6 eggs on high speed 1 min until foamy. Gradually add 1 cup sugar then continue beating on high for 8 min. It will be whipped and forming thick ribbons when you pull up the whisk.
In a separate bowl, whisk together 1 cup flour and 1/2 tsp baking powder.

Sift flour into batter 1/3 at a time, folding between each addition, just until no flour streaks remain. Scrape from the bottom to catch any hidden flour pockets. Divide evenly between prepared cake pans and bake at 350°F for 23-28 min (my oven takes 25 min). Tops should be golden brown and spring back when poked lightly.
Run a knife or thin spatula around edges to loosen and invert onto wire rack. Peel back parchment paper right away and let cakes cool right-side-up to room temp before cutting them in half.
How to Make Cream Cheese Frosting:
In the bowl of a stand mixer fitted with whisk attachment, combine 16 oz cream cheese, 1 cup butter, 2 1/2 cups powdered sugar and 2 tsp vanilla. Beat on low to combine then increase to high and beat 5-6 mins, scraping down the bowl as needed. Frosting should be whipped, soft and spreadable. Transfer 1 cup frosting to piping bag fitted with large open star tip and refrigerate until ready to use for the topping.
How to Cut Mango:

A mango has one long, flat seed in the center of the fruit that goes from stem to nose. Slice off the sides around the seeds of all 4 whole mangos resulting in 8 halves. Set aside 4 halves - you will need them to decorate the top. Dice remaining 4 halves and scoop them out of their skin then transfer these to a blender and process until puréed. Taste the mango purée and add sugar to taste if needed.
How to Assemble the Mango Cake:
Place the first sliced cake layer on a platter and spread with 1/2 cup mango purée. On the second cake layer, spread 1/2 cup frosting and place it frosting-side-down on the first layer so the cream and mango are hugging. Repeat with remaining layers then cover top and sides with remaining frosting. Pipe reserved frosting around the top border of your cake.
Peel and thinly slice 4 reserved mango halves, cutting some strips long way and some wide. Layer mango slices in rings around the cake, starting with the longest pieces and overlapping each piece slightly until only a 1/2" space is left in the center. Roll a long thin strip of mango into a coil and place it in the center. Cake can be served right away or refrigerated 2 hours for easier slicing. It keeps well covered and refrigerated up to 3 days.

Lemon Mousse Cake

Ingredients
US Customary – Metric
FOR LEMON CAKE:
1 cup unsalted butter, softened
1 cup white granulated sugar
2 teaspoons lemon extract
4 large eggs
1 cup milk
2 cups all-purpose flour
4 teaspoons baking powder
1/2 teaspoon salt
zest from 2 large lemons
For Lemon Curd:
2/3 cup freshly-squeezed lemon juice
2 eggs
4 egg yolks
1 cup white granulated sugar
1/2 cup unsalted butter
1 tsp vanilla extract

FOR MOUSSE:
3 cups heavy cream, chilled
1 1/2 cups confectioner's sugar
1 tsp lemon extract
yellow food coloring, optional
4 tsp unflavored gelatin
2 tbsp water

FOR JELLO:
3 oz package lemon jello
1/2 cup boiling water
1/2 cup ice

Instructions

Preheat the oven to 350/177C. This recipe will make a three-layer cake using 8-inch cake pans and a two-layer cake using 9-inch cake pans. Line the pans with parchment paper and spray the sides with a baking spray.

Prepare the lemon cake: In a large mixing bowl, beat together softened butter, sugar and lemon extract for a few minutes until fluffy. Add the eggs and beat again until creamy and smooth, about 2 to 3 minutes. Next, pour in the milk but don't mix it in yet (I recommend using warm milk). In a separate bowl, combine all the dry ingredients: flour, baking powder and salt. Sift the dry ingredients into the cake batter and whisk in the dry ingredients and milk by hand to avoid over-mixing the batter. Add the lemon zest last and fold it in gently.

Divide the cake batter evenly between the prepared pans. Bake in preheated oven for approximately 30 minutes or until a toothpick inserted into the center comes out clean. Allow the cake layers to cool completely on a wire rack, then use a long, serrated knife to level off the tops. Place the cake layers into the freezer for faster cooling.

While the cake layers are baking, prepare the lemon curd. Juice approximately 4 to 5 large lemons over a fine mesh strainer set up over a glass bowl or large measuring cup. Double strain the juice for smoothest lemon curd. Set juice aside. In a small stainless steel pot, combine the eggs, egg yolks and sugar. Whisk vigorously for 3 to 4 minutes, until the mixture is thick and more pale in color: it should ribbon off the whisk. Add the lemon juice and whisk to combine.

Cook the lemon curd over medium-low heat, stirring constantly along the bottom of the pan with a rubber spatula. Cook for 4 to 5 minutes, until the curd thickens and starts to bubble lightly. Remove from heat immediately. Add the unsalted butter and vanilla and whisk until the butter is completely melted, then cover the lemon curd. Allow the lemon filling to cool slightly, then place into the refrigerator. Place into the freezer to cool faster.

Once the lemon curd and lemon cake layers are COMPLETELY cooled, prepare the mousse. Pour the chilled heavy cream into a large mixer bowl and add the sugar and lemon extract. Whisk on high speed for 3 to 4 minutes, until stiff peaks form. Reserve approximately 1 cup of the resulting whipped cream for garnishing the top. Add the chilled lemon curd to the whipped cream: reserve 1/2 cup of the lemon curd for spreading onto the cake layers. Whisk on medium speed for about 1 minute.

Prepare the gelatin: place the unflavored gelatin and water into a small bowl and stir to combine. Microwave the gelatin for 30 to 40 seconds, stirring often, until the gelatin is completely dissolved. With the mixer running on medium speed, pour the HOT gelatin into the mousse. Do not wait for the gelatin to cool: it will form clumps! Mix the mousse for another minute on medium speed until the mousse is uniform and smooth. Watch my video recipe to see how it's done.

To assemble the cake: line the sides of an 8-inch or 9-inch (depending on the size of your cake layers) with an acetate cake collar (link in post). A double layer of foil will work in a pinch. Make sure to the acetate collar overlaps a few inches to prevent the jello from pouring out! Spread a few tablespoons of the reserved lemon curd onto each cake layer. Place the first cake layer into the springform pan, then add 3 cups of the mousse. Spread it evenly to the edges with a spoon, then add the second layer. Repeat this process again, leveling the top layer of mousse as much as possible. Place the cake into the refrigerator to chill for 1 hour.

Prepare the lemon jello topping: in a measuring cup or small bowl, combine the flavored gelatin with 1/2 cup boiling water (this is half the recommended amount) and stir for a few minutes until the gelatin is completely dissolved. If needed, microwave the mixture for 30 seconds to dissolve completely. Add 1/2 cup ice cubes to cool the jello down. The mixture needs to be cool before pouring over the mousse. After the mousse cake has set for 1 hour, gently pour the jello over the top.

Refrigerate the lemon cake for an additional 6 to 8 hours, or overnight. When ready to enjoy, remove the springform and use a cake spatula to transfer the cake onto a stand. Remove the plastic acetate when ready to serve. Add dollops of the reserved whipped cream on top: I used an open French star tip #4. To prevent the cake from drying out, keep it wrapped in the plastic cake collar while refrigerated.

Hummingbird Cake

Ingredients

For the Cake:

16 ounces canned crushed pineapple in juice
3 cups (360 g) all-purpose flour
2 teaspoons baking powder
1 teaspoon baking soda
1 teaspoon salt
1 teaspoon ground cinnamon
2 cups (396 g) granulated sugar
3 eggs
1 cup (198 g) vegetable oil
4 very ripe large bananas, peeled and mashed (about 2 cups)
1½ cup (171 g) pecans, toasted and chopped
2 teaspoons vanilla extract

For the Frosting:

1¼ cups (283 g) unsalted butter, at room temperature
5 cups (568 g) powdered sugar
2½ teaspoons vanilla extract

½ teaspoon salt
20 ounces (567 g) cream cheese, chilled and cut into 20 pieces

To Garnish:

½ cup (57 g) pecans, toasted and chopped

Instructions

Make the Cake: Preheat oven to 350 degrees F. Grease three 8-inch cake pans (you can also do two 9-inch pans), line the bottoms with parchment paper, grease the parchment and flour the pans; set aside.

Drain the pineapple in a fine-mesh strainer set over a small saucepan, pressing to remove as much juice as possible. Place the saucepan over medium heat until reduced to ⅓ cup, about 5 minutes; set aside.

In a medium bowl, whisk together the flour, baking powder, baking soda, cinnamon and salt.

In a large bowl, whisk together the sugar and eggs, then whisk in the oil. Using a rubber spatula, stir in the bananas, pecans, vanilla, drained pineapple, and reduced pineapple juice. Gently stir in the flour mixture until just combined.

Divide the batter evenly between the prepared pans and smooth the tops with a spatula. Bake until dark golden brown on top and a toothpick inserted in the center comes out clean, 35 to 40 minutes (a little less for the 9-inch pans), rotating the pans halfway through baking. Let the cakes cool in pans on a wire rack for 20 minutes, then turn out of the pans, remove parchment paper and allow to cool completely, at least 2 hours.

Make the Frosting: Using an electric mixer, beat the butter, sugar, vanilla and salt on low speed until smooth, then mix for an additional 2 minutes, scraping down the bowl as needed. Increase the speed to medium-low and add the cream cheese one piece at a time and mix until smooth, then mix for an additional 2 minutes.

Place one cake layer on a serving platter. Spread 1 cup of frosting over top, then top with another cake layer, pressing lightly to adhere. Spread another 1 cups of frosting over that layer, then top with the third cake layer. Spread the remaining frosting evenly over the sides and top of the cake. Sprinkle the top of the cake with the chopped pecans. Refrigerate for at least 1 hour before serving. The cake can be stored in the refrigerator for up to 2 days.

Vegan simnel cake

Ingredients

200ml soya milk

1 lemon, zested and ½ juiced

500g marzipan

icing sugar, for dusting

250g dairy-free spread, plus extra for the tin

250g mixed dried fruit (we used sultanas, raisins and candied peel)

75g glacé cherries, roughly chopped

1 orange, zested and juiced

200g light brown soft sugar

200g plain flour

75g ground almonds

1 tsp baking powder

½ tsp ground ginger

½ tsp ground cinnamon

1 tsp mixed spice

2 tsp vanilla bean paste

25g apricot jam, warmed, plus extra for sticking the marzipan balls to the cake

Method

Mix the soya milk with the lemon juice in a jug and set aside for a few minutes to thicken. Cut 150g of the marzipan from the larger block. Roll this out on a work surface lightly dusted with icing sugar until it's just slightly smaller than the base of a 23cm cake tin. Using the dairy-free spread, butter a 23cm springform cake tin and line with a double layer of baking parchment. Heat the oven to 180C/160C fan/gas 4.

Mix the dried fruit, lemon zest, chopped cherries and orange zest and juice together in a large bowl, tossing a few times until well combined.

Beat the vegan spread with the brown sugar until pale using an electric whisk, then add the flour, almonds, baking powder, spices and vanilla. Tip in the milk mixture until you have a smooth batter. Fold in the fruit along with a pinch of salt and any juice from the bowl until well combined – don't worry if the batter looks slightly curdled.

Spoon half the batter into the prepared tin, then gently smooth the surface with the back of the spoon and top with the round of marzipan. Spoon over the remaining batter and smooth the surface again. Bake for 30 mins, then reduce the oven to 150C/130C fan/gas 2 and bake for another 1 hr 45 mins-2 hrs, or until a skewer comes out clean and the cake is well-risen and firm. Carefully remove from the tin and leave to cool completely on a wire rack. Cut into slices to serve. Will keep for two weeks in an airtight container.

Brush the warm apricot jam over the cooled cake. Cut a 200g piece from the remaining marzipan and roll it out again as before. Cut out a 23cm circle using the base of the cake tin as a guide. Use the rolling pin to help you lift the marzipan circle over the cake and gently press it onto the surface (the apricot jam will help it stick). Divide the remaining marzipan into 11 pieces and roll into balls. Use a little more jam to stick the balls around the edge of the cake – these represent the 12 apostles, minus Judas. If you like, use a kitchen blowtorch to slightly burnish the marzipan balls and topping until just golden (do this carefully so they don't burn).

Apricot and Almond fruit cake

Ingredients
140g golden sultana
4 tbsp sherry
250g pack butter, softened, plus extra for greasing
250g light soft brown sugar
1 tsp vanilla extract
3 large eggs, beaten
200g plain flour
1 tsp baking powder
100g ground almond
50g toasted flaked almond
140g dried apricot, chopped
140g mixed peel
zest and juice 1 lemon
zest and juice 1 orange

Method

Mix the sultanas and sherry and set aside for 1 hr to soak.
Heat oven to 160C/140C fan/gas 3. Grease a deep, 23cm loose-bottomed cake tin, and line the base and sides with a double layer of baking parchment that comes about 2.5cm above the sides of the tin. In your largest mixing bowl, beat the butter, sugar and vanilla together until pale and fluffy. Beat in the eggs one by one.
g76î/vb˚-2esî7ṭ0-sbn/7puba="W_aEq-)Stir in the flour, baking poṭwder, and the ground and flaked almonds. Next, add the soaked sultanas with any remaining sherry, the dried apricots, the mixed peel, and all the zest and juice. Scrape into the cake tin, smoothing out the surface.

Bake on the middle shelf of the oven for 1 hr 25 mins. Poke with a skewer in the centre to check it is cooked – if the skewer comes out with any uncooked mixture stuck to it, bake for 10 mins more before checking again. Cool in the tin. Decorated, or wrapped in greaseproof paper and foil, the cake will keep for up to a month.

Salted caramel pear cake

Ingredients
2cm piece ginger, grated
4 Williams pears, 3 grated over a sieve, reserving the pear juice for the caramel, 1
peeled, cored and chopped (do this when about to decorate)
360g self-raising flour
15g rye flour
1 tsp ground ginger
½ tsp turmeric
½ tsp nutmeg
½ tsp ground cardamom
½ tsp cinnamon
1 tsp baking powder
4 eggs
200g golden caster sugar
150g light brown muscovado sugar, sieved
150ml rapeseed or vegetable oil
120g natural yogurt
toasted buckwheat, dehydrated pear and rosemary, to serve (optional)
For the pear-salted caramel
50g unsalted butter, plus extra for the tins
50ml reserved pear juice
150ml perry
100g light brown muscovado sugar
1 tbsp double cream
generous pinch sea salt
For the icing
4 egg whites
250g golden caster sugar
250g butter, at room temperature
2 tbsp tahini
1 tbsp vanilla bean paste

Method

Heat oven to 195C/175C fan/gas 5 ½. Butter and line the base of three 20cm round cake tins. Add the grated ginger to the grated pear and push down with a wooden spoon to squeeze out as much juice as possible.

Mix the flours, spices, baking powder and 1 tsp salt in a bowl. In a stand mixer, vigorously whisk the eggs and sugars for 3 mins until thick and frothy. Slowly pour in the oil in a steady stream. Turn the speed down, then add the flour mixture, 2 tbsp at a time, alternating with the yogurt, until incorporated. Mix in the grated pear (for no longer than 20 secs). Divide the mixture between the tins and bake for 25-30 mins or until a skewer inserted comes out dry.

For the caramel, heat the pear juice and perry in a pan until reduced to about 50ml. Add the sugar and butter and whisk to a smooth caramel, then add the cream and whisk again until smooth. Add sea salt to your taste – I'd go for a generous pinch, so that the caramel is still fruity and sharp but has a little saltiness to it – then allow to cool slightly to just warmer than room temperature.

To make the buttercream, put the egg whites and sugar in the bowl of a stand mixer. Place the bowl over a pan of boiling water, then whisk until the sugar dissolves and the mixture is no longer gritty. Put the bowl in the mixer, then whisk until soft peaks form and the bowl returns to room temperature. Switch to the paddle attachment, then add the butter, one spoonful at a time. Add the tahini, vanilla and a pinch of salt, and beat to a light, fluffy icing.

Place the bottom layer of sponge on a platter or cake stand, then top with a layer of the buttercream and scatter over a third of the chopped pear. Repeat with the next two layers. To ice the cake, do an intial layer all over, chill in the fridge for 20 mins, then use the remaining icing to cover everything. Use a stepped spatula to spread it out evenly. Pour the caramel over the top of the cake, and allow it to drip down the sides. Scatter with toasted buckwheat, dehydrated pear and rosemary, if you like.

Thank you for choosing to embark on this culinary journey with me and for entrusting me with a small part of your kitchen adventures.

Your support and trust mean the world to me. Every recipe, every technique, and every story shared in this cookbook is a reflection of my passion for food and my desire to bring joy to your tables. Your decision to purchase this cookbook not only encourages me to continue sharing my culinary knowledge but also supports the countless hours of recipe testing, writing, and photography that went into its creation.

Wishing you many happy moments of deliciousness and culinary creativity!

For Zian And Milan,who brings smiles to my face and joy to my heart every day